Outside Looking In

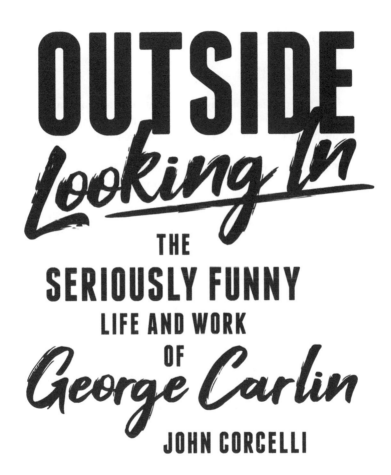

OUTSIDE
Looking In

THE
SERIOUSLY FUNNY
LIFE AND WORK
OF
George Carlin

JOHN CORCELLI

APPLAUSE
THEATRE & CINEMA BOOKS

Essex, Connecticut

APPLAUSE
THEATRE & CINEMA BOOKS

An imprint of Globe Pequot, the trade division of
The Rowman & Littlefield Publishing Group, Inc.
4501 Forbes Blvd., Ste. 200
Lanham, MD 20706
www.rowman.com

Distributed by NATIONAL BOOK NETWORK

Library of Congress Cataloging-in-Publication Data

Names: Corcelli, John, author.
Title: Outside looking in : the seriously funny life and work of George Carlin / John Corcelli.
Identifiers: LCCN 2022024488 (print) | LCCN 2022024489 (ebook) | ISBN 9781493062201
   (cloth) | ISBN 9781493062218 (ebook)
Subjects: LCSH: Carlin, George. | Comedians—United States—Biography. | Actors—United
   States—Biography. | Stand-up comedy—United States—History.
Classification: LCC PN2287.C2685 C67 2022 (print) | LCC PN2287.C2685 (ebook) | DDC
   792.7/6028092 [B]—dc23/eng/20220725
LC record available at https://lccn.loc.gov/2022024488
LC ebook record available at https://lccn.loc.gov/2022024489

In memory of Louie Anderson, Gilbert Gottfried, Tony Hendra, Norm Macdonald, Paul Mooney, Mort Sahl, and my mother.

"The privilege of a lifetime is to become who you truly are."

—C. G. Jung

CONTENTS

Acknowledgments

Nobody succeeds without the help of others, and so it was for me on this extraordinary journey into the life of George Carlin written during the COVID-19 pandemic. So it is with great appreciation, gratitude, indebtedness, and high regard that I recognize a few individuals in addition to thanking my family. First, special thanks to my wife, Helena, for her patience and support in my quest to write the best book possible about my favorite comedian. *You* are my favorite. Second, big hugs to Donald Brackett, Paul Kaliciak, and Dan Reynish for their comments on the original pitch that impressed John Cerullo at Rowman & Littlefield back in 2020. Thanks John! And to Chris Chappell, Barbara Claire, Laurel Myers, Della Vaché, and Sally Rinehart at R&L.

Mark Rheaume played a significant role in recommending books with the best portraits of Lenny Bruce and Richard Pryor, among others. Mark's savant memory of television shows saved me from the rabbit hole that is the internet. To Tim Keele, whose keen insights regarding Lenny Bruce and the First Amendment to the U.S. Constitution helped shaped the narrative regarding freedom of speech. He also provided excellent feedback on selected chapters. Thanks to Bobby Tanzilo for going the extra mile regarding Carlin's bust in Milwaukee in 1972.

And to Laurie Abkemeier, Dr. Stephanie Adams, Carlen Altman, T. J. Beitelman, Stephen Book, Cara Cockrum, Edwin Dumont,

Suzanne Friedman, Fermand Garlington, Joe Mahoney, Tom Metuzals, Bev Reid, Joey Reynolds, Scott Saul, Judith and Laurence Siegel, Alicia Van Couvering, Terry Vosbein, Gretchen Young, Richard Zoglin, Barrie Zwicker, and the staff at the Toronto Public Library for responding to my questions in a timely fashion. You made a difference.

Introduction

> I [now] reside out where the Oort cloud is, where the comets gather, and from that perspective, I have no stake in the game and I can really make my commentary mean something. (*Charlie Rose*, PBS, 1992)

In 1972, when I was fourteen years of age, my brother Mike brought home a copy of George Carlin's album *Class Clown*. He borrowed it from the older brother of a friend of ours. This was a high-risk moment in our house one sunny afternoon. Our mother was preparing dinner, and we played the record on our new Rogers Majestic Home stereo unit. It took center stage in the living room of our suburban bungalow. If you know the album, the dangerous side is side 2 for Carlin's "Seven Words You Can Never Say on Television," and you can't say them or hear them in the living room before dinner either.

But side 1 had fart jokes perfectly suited as family entertainment. Carlin called it "Bi-Labial Fricative": the sound your lips make as you blow against your arm. As the record played, I could hear my mother laughing from the kitchen. Clearly, the class clown found his audience of one, plus two teenagers looking to hear side 2 as soon as possible. It was an important connection between the three of us. Who would have thought that a bunch of fart jokes would carry the day?

George Carlin was a self-imposed outsider. Yet he somehow was the ultimate insider. In my first book on Frank Zappa (*All That's*

Left to Know About the Father of Invention, 2016), I looked at a man who took rock music in a serious direction that was often comedic; Carlin, on the other hand, experimented with the prevailing customs of comedy, taking satire in a direction that was very serious indeed. From his Oort cloud vantage point, Carlin could observe and report with biting wit.

Carlin's comic art was entertaining, thoughtful, and frightening. He loved words, and the words often came easily. He lived from 1937 until 2008, with the bulk of those seventy-one years dedicated to entertaining people with words. He "killed it" in the trade's vernacular. Today, he's considered one the most important stand-up comedians. He transformed the art from simple joke telling to insightful social commentary. Carlin made you laugh, but he also made you think.

George Carlin's life and work were in a state of constant revision. His writing demanded it, and his family relied on it. He was a steady worker continually focused on crafting the perfect joke, one-liner, or diatribe. When an idea struck him, he wrote it down as soon as possible. If a catchphrase from a newscast or headline grabbed him, he grabbed his pen and wrote it down to be stored for later use. He was a hoarder of words, some of which were obscene.

Obscene words, Marshall McLuhan once said, "hit you in the midriff." George Carlin was not the first comedian to use profanity in his act. He simply used it to emphasize a point, a percussive instrument in his arsenal. John McWhorter, in his excellent book *Nine Nasty Words* published in 2021, suggests that as humans, "profanity channels our essence without always making sense." Carlin spent the bulk of his life trying to make sense of how we use language. His goal was to deconstruct words, peel back their meanings, and disarm them of their power. But he could get only so far. After all, he was a performer, not a linguist.

That said, Carlin was an effective artist whose powers of persuasion made you laugh. When he made the conscious decision to step back from the world and assume a perch to watch "the freak show," as he called it, he could see the big picture and consider all the weird shit humans do—and then, like a mirror, reflect it back to us in the form of a well-conceived joke.

In writing this book, my focus has been to step back and watch *his* show. His body of work rivals some of the finest comedians of our age. Over time, I concluded that Carlin's life as an artist may be seen as an evolving arc: class clown, jester, poet, and philosopher. "Arc" has a particular meaning here: it's something with an identifiable beginning and end but one that curves and does not follow the straightest, shortest line. Carlin ended up as a hugely successful comedian, but his path was not always a direct one.

He didn't do it alone. Along the way, he had help from family, friends, and a few nuns. He suffered loss. He got hooked on drugs, then recovered. He was arrested twice, and he almost went bankrupt. But he persevered, fueled by the laughter he could generate with a wisecrack or a fart joke capped with a profound observation. As he matured, he became wiser, sharper, and more attuned to the human condition, even though it left him disappointed and disillusioned most of the time. As he described humanity to Sonny Fox on XM Radio in 2006, "I think this was a species that was given great gifts and had great potential and squandered them."

So what was he to do? The only thing he could do: make fun of it.

Jesus is coming . . . look busy. BONNIE FROM KENDALL PARK, NJ, USA/WIKIMEDIA
COMMONS

Class Clown (1937-1961)

One

A Comedian Is Born

*I*t's painful to imagine the world of comedy without George Carlin, but it almost happened.

When Mary Carlin, George's mother, became pregnant at forty, she considered the consequences. Her husband, Patrick Carlin Sr., was forty-eight and completely unreliable. He drank whiskey like it was an elixir for his health and was seldom home. He didn't want to be responsible for another mouth to feed. Mary was in an awful marriage, but she loved Pat and would always give her husband a second chance—and a third and a fourth.

Pat and Mary were star-crossed lovers at the time of their sexual union in the summer of 1936, one of the few times they agreed on anything. As George liked to say, he was conceived on a sultry August night in Curley's Hotel in Rockaway Beach, New York. The beach was a favorite location for young people to party in those days. In fact, the pair had been separated for two years when they got reacquainted on the street one day. On a whim, he asked her to go to Rockaway Beach, and she agreed because what brought Mary and Pat together, despite his volatility and their long separation, was their irresistible sexual attraction. She was caught up in a dysfunctional relationship in which she had limited control, especially when Pat got violent. Carlin remembers his father hit his mother only once, but his older brother, Patrick Jr., born in 1931, said it happened to him and to her regularly. Mary's father, Dennis Bearey, was a New York Police Department officer she often called on for help.

Patrick John Carlin was born in the town of Donegal, Ireland, in 1888. He was older than George's mother, Mary Bearey, born in New York in 1895. They were married in 1930—her first marriage and his second. After the birth of Patrick Jr., Pat Sr. was serious about not having another child, so he and Mary paid a visit to a high-priced "specialist" in Gramercy Square. He went by the pseudonym Dr. Sunshine, and he was skilled in the surgical treatment called dilation and curettage (D&C for short). To this day, it is the most common surgical procedure for terminating pregnancies in the United States. But in 1936, it was available only to those who could pay for it; Pat Carlin had the financial means because he was a successful ad salesperson for the *New York Evening Post*. On the chosen day, while the couple was sitting outside the operating room, Mary Carlin had what her future second son described as a "vision." Apparently, she had seen an image of her recently deceased mother in a painting on the wall of the waiting room that changed her mind. Mary took control, telling Pat that she was going to keep the baby. He went to a local saloon and got pissed.

George Denis Patrick Carlin arrived on May 12, 1937, with his first name chosen in honor of Mary's brother. He was born ten years and one day after legendary comedian Mort Sahl and less than a week after the airship *Hindenburg* blew up on arrival at the Lakehurst Naval Station in New Jersey. To say that the advent of George Carlin did not make headlines at the time wouldn't surprise anyone. But for the world of comedy, a member of what Jon Stewart affectionately called the "holy trinity of stand-up" was born. (The other two? Lenny Bruce and Richard Pryor.)

Pat had worked for the original *New York Evening Post*, which was renamed the *New York Post* in 1934. (Rupert Murdoch purchased the newspaper in 1976 and changed the format from a broadsheet to a tabloid.) As national advertising manager, Carlin filled the big pages of the paper with ads generating revenue. As the money poured in, Pat gained his notoriety on Madison Avenue. As a salesman, he was an excellent communicator.

In the 1930s, when a majority of American workers were lining up for soup, Carlin's father prospered. He earned a salary plus commission at the *Post* while holding a part-time job as a public speaker. He earned up to $1,000 a week entertaining paying audiences with *The Power of Mental Demand*, one of the earliest versions of motivational speeches decades before Tony Robbins made the scene. The speech was from a book published in 1913, one of a collection of ten pieces edited by Herbert Edward Law. All its essays focus on the elements of success in business and in life from the perspective of flourishing businesspeople. Among the claims in the preface is the notion that "success must come from one's own self."

Depending on one's point of view, *The Power of Mental Demand* reads like a sales pitch. Its dense, precise language unfolds like a passage from a Calvinist tract, but the basic message is positive and inspiring, just the words that an audience needed to hear during the Depression: "We are the creatures of destiny; but our destiny is within us. It must be achieved by our own effort." The essay also talks about the ingredients needed to be successful such as "focus, concentration, intention and will" four words that would have a strong association with George's future as a dynamic comedian. In 1935, Pat won the Dale Carnegie National Public Speaking Contest, beating more than 800 contestants at the Waldorf Astoria. George kept the gavel they awarded his father as a keepsake.

So when George was born, his father earned more than enough to support his wife, two sons, and a Black maid named Amanda on tony Riverside Drive in New York. The building is now known as the Vauxhall, a few steps away from the Hudson River at the corner of

155th Street. The Carlin family lived in modest comfort during the Depression, but it didn't last long.

Unfortunately, Pat senior's success did not translate into domestic bliss. In later years, George often told the story of his great escape from his father's clutches while in the arms of his mother. Hiding out one time in his grandfather's apartment during one of Pat's drinking spells, Mary, Patrick, and George were discovered by the elder Carlin. They collected their things, rushed down the fire escape to Broadway and into the car of Mary's brother Tom, and fled to the countryside. They rarely saw Pat again. As strict Catholics, divorce was out of the question, so Mary legally separated from Patrick Sr., and by the fall of 1937, she was a single parent with a six-year-old and an infant. She took charge of her family, got a job at the Association of National Advertisers, and looked for a new home where her bully of a husband couldn't find her and the boys. For the next few years, Mary, Patrick, and George lived like ramblers, seeking a safe and affordable place to live. Eventually, Mary found a small apartment on West 121st Street in Morningside Heights for the three of them in 1941.

Even though Carlin barely knew his father, he still felt "a profound connection" to his dad based on his father's accomplishments. In his posthumous memoir *Last Words* (2009), Carlin described Pat as someone with a broad outlook, one that encompassed "his own relationship to the universe at large." The picture Carlin had of his father was largely gleaned from his mother's and brother's memories: a man who was charming when sober but violent when drunk.

In 1990, Carlin discovered something about his father that he never knew: he had been in recovery at a monastery of the Graymoor Friars in Garrison, New York, three years after George was born. The information came to him from his half sister, Mary, the product of Pat's first marriage. Mary shared a letter from her father written in 1941 that revealed his new, unpaid job as a kitchen assistant to Brother Capistran at the monastery. Carlin Sr., despite his past financial success, wound up sharing the same space and food as the priests and clergy members in the monastery. Today, the congregation is known as the Society of Atonement, remaining an active center for seekers of faith and sobriety. Perhaps it was Pat's form of penance to get sober, heeding the content from his own speeches in *The Power of Mental Demand*. He died of a heart attack at fifty-seven. Fifteen years after learning this story, George would seek sobriety for himself at a facility in Malibu, California, at a place called Promises.

With no father figure in the house, Mary became the central force in the lives of her children. In his memoir, Carlin says she imposed her strong will and ideals on her two sons intensely, pushing them to fall in line with her way of thinking (*Last Words*). Tony Hendra, a close friend of Carlin's, said, "I think her dream for him was to have become a nice, sober, successful version of her husband" (*A&E Biography*, April 12, 2000).

Mary played favorites. In her mind, Patrick wasn't up to snuff (George often overheard his mother berating his brother), but George was a winner, and she pushed him to succeed. For a couple of summers, George went to Camp Notre Dame, a Catholic resort in New Hampshire on Spofford Lake near the town of Keene. The operation was much like a boot camp for boys aged six to sixteen in the perfect setting, Mary thought, for some male supervision. The seasonal fee was $185 for a nine-week stay. Carlin thrived here under a program that included not only athletics, such as basketball and canoeing, but also drama and storytelling. They held mass every morning before the real fun began. One summer, Carlin won a medal for a dramatic performance. He cherished the embossed Sock and Buskin prize on a chain and wore it around his neck for the rest of his life.

Growing up, the brothers loved each other because Patrick was George's role model. He went to a Catholic boarding school called

Mount Saint Michael from the age of seven to eleven, and George saw his brother only on Easter Sunday and at Christmas during those formative years. Despite the infrequent visits, they remained close, and the six-year difference in their ages was an advantage to George, the younger. One time when George learned an unfamiliar word that he heard as "cow-sucker," Patrick corrected his four-year-old brother: it was pronounced "cocksucker." As an adult, Patrick would become a valuable ally in support of his brother's art, notably the darker humor of his later years. For example, his brother's bold look at the world reinforced his 2001 piece "I Kinda Like It When a Lotta People Die." Perhaps it was his resilience as a youth in the face of violence from either his father or the priests at boarding school that hit him. Patrick was one tough kid. He died on April 16, 2022. In *Variety*, his niece Kelly described him as "a tough mofo."

Mary Carlin was not only George's biggest fan; she was his first artistic director. When he was six, she taught him how to entertain people at her workplace by imitating Mae West and "Johnny the Bellboy," a mascot for Philip Morris, the cigarette maker, showcasing Carlin's particular ability to mimic the sounds of the people he heard in his neighborhood and in popular culture. Mary also taught him a dance called the "Big Apple" named after the South Carolina venue in which it originated in the early 1930s. By 1937, the dance was a massive craze in dance halls across the United States. *Life* magazine reported the story in several issues that year, featuring pictures from the Manhattan Room in New York's Hotel Pennsylvania. The superb images reveal one of the hot spots where young people could go all out on the dance floor.

Carlin attended the Corpus Christi primary school, steps away from his home on West 121st Street. Father Ford, an ecumenist, led the school and espoused John Dewey's model of progressive education. The school was coed, requiring no uniforms, and it did not issue report cards. Most noteworthy, there was no corporal punishment.

Corpus Christi Catholic Church, New York. Steps away from Carlin's home.

For a Catholic school, this was highly unusual. Yet these experimental settings freed up the students. Once a month, a priest would visit his class in what Carlin later called "Heavy Mystery Time." They encouraged the students to ask questions about the existence of God and why Catholics don't eat meat on Good Friday. He learned a lot of things under the umbrella of religion but felt no connection to the doctrine. "If we were inculcated with anything," he writes in his memoir, "it was the simple idea that the future would take care of itself if you did right by yourself today." This "simple idea" provided Carlin with a sense that he could think for himself, being resilient in the face of authority or dismissive of a system of beliefs.

The freedom of the classroom was a double-edged sword for Carlin. On the one hand, he could daydream about the world unfolding before him and ask questions. He felt limited by the answers found in the Catholic principles laid down by the nuns and priests who taught him. "The disrespect I had for the dogmatic aspect and for the inconsistency and cruelty of the Catholic doctrine," he told James Lipton, "was tempered with an affection and a gratitude that I had for this wonderful setting. I considered it like a garden where they let me grow" (*Inside the Actors Studio*, Bravo, October 31, 2004).

To stem the boredom, Carlin took on a new role: class clown. It took guts. You needed to make kids laugh without being caught by the teacher, whose back was usually turned when you went to work. As class clown, you had to be a show-off and attention seeker, two of Carlin's fundamental needs at ten years of age. He also had a stockpile of physical tricks, such as cracking his knuckles, strange facial expressions, and the all-purpose fart sounds. It was his way of pushing the limits of a system that expected him to conform.

Since his mom often worked a demanding schedule that ran late, Carlin had an interval of several hours to himself after school. Not a lot of kids could say that in the late 1940s. For them, Dad went to work, and Mom stayed home. So, if he wasn't running with the troublemakers as a kid, he listened to rhythm-and-blues records, dreaming of becoming a disk jockey. He filled his time reading comics and magazines. Among his favorites at the time were *Ballyhoo*, a humor magazine created in 1931, and a monthly called *1000 Jokes*, published by Dell featuring single-panel cartoons and parody. At age twelve, he had a subscription to the music magazine *Downbeat*. Carlin's book collection included one of his most cherished, *Esar's Comic Dictionary*, published by Harvest House in 1943. It presented new interpretations of words and phrases by American literary humorist Evan Esar. Here's one of thousands in the work: "Public speaking is the art of diluting a two-minute idea with a two-hour vocabulary." Carlin would take an opposite approach: he studied the art of making jokes concisely and effectively as much as he could, amassing a skill set that no school, be it primary or secondary, could provide.

Carlin also had his radio to console him long before television took over the home. He listened to *The Lone Ranger*, *Fibber McGee and Molly*, and variety show hosts Fred Allen and Henry Morgan, who had an enormous impact on him. Allen was an eminently successful writer and satirist during the so-called golden age of radio. The Library of Congress holds 400 of his radio scripts in its collection. Henry Morgan, one of radio's first irreverent hosts and stars, took to improvising his lines during a live broadcast, usually taking shots at sponsors. Carlin was such a huge fan that he collected autographs from his favorite radio stars at the RCA building. Comics, magazines, radio—it was a marvelous time for the latchkey kid.

By the fifth grade, at age eleven, Carlin was identifying himself as a performer beyond the classroom and his mother's secretary pool. At one point, he had to submit an assignment to his teacher describing what he wanted to do when he grew up. Carlin's answer was sharp and poignant, laying out his preferred options: "actor, impersonator, comedian, disk jockey, announcer, or trumpet player" (*Last Words*). The last question wasn't unusual, but Carlin's answer certainly was. Most kids at eleven choose popular occupations, such as police officer, doctor, or firefighter, your standard civil service jobs. But not young George Carlin. He was identifying his own path as a self-described "pure hambone-entertainer child-show off," an occupation he later spelled out as "Foole."

When he wasn't at Camp Notre Dame, one of Carlin's favorite locations during the summer, as it was for many New Yorkers, was Coney Island—a south Brooklyn amusement park built in the nineteenth century featuring a beach, a beautiful boardwalk, and rides. The site also featured Voice-O-Graphs built by International Mutoscope in 1940. These small recording units were vertical structures made of wood, about the size of a telephone booth, with a microphone and a soundproof door. A person could record up to sixty seconds of their own voice for twenty-five cents; the device would inscribe the audio on a record and deliver it to you when you were done. Carlin and his friend Teddy Dibble made some telling and delightful records in 1947. They are included on the seven-disc set *George Carlin: The Little David Years* released in 1999 on Atlantic.

The "Coney Island Recordings" feature more than seven minutes' worth of newscasts, sports scores, songs, and police bulletins, all delivered by your host, George Carlin. What we hear today are not simple novelty recordings; they are audio gold. They reveal an enthusiastic kid performing his own stuff albeit emulating the tone of contemporary radio newscasts he learned at home. But the boy had energy, charm, and a knack for hitting the punch line. These recordings represent the earliest version of the class clown in performance: a natural voice working the crowd and entertaining us with one-minute bits, incorporating sound effects produced by Teddy Dibble. They reveal a friendly, fearless, and talented performer ready to try anything to make you laugh. In the liner notes, Carlin recalls the experience: "You may have had some ideas when you began, but pretty soon they ran out, and you were on your own, clutching at every stale bit and ad-lib you could think of." On these early recordings, we hear Carlin's impressions of some of his movie heroes: Peter Lorre, James Cagney, Humphrey Bogart, and, perhaps less amusingly for modern audiences, Brother Bones, a caricature of a Black preacher.

When Carlin graduated from Corpus Christi in 1950, his mom gave him a Webcor reel-to-reel tape machine. At thirteen years of age, the class clown now had his own home studio to record anything he wished and for longer than a minute. He used it all the time, recording stories of the personalities he heard on the street corners of his neighborhood. He mimicked local accents and the voices of the nuns and priests at Corpus Christi. Soon, he was being called on to entertain his older brother's friends at house parties. The class clown was taking his show on the road and garnering laughs.

After grade school, Carlin started at Cardinal Hayes High School in The Bronx. It was here, in 1951, that Carlin started smoking marijuana with his brother. In those days, passing a joint was more fun than attending classes. That, along with his scrappy defiance of authority, distinguished him from most of the other students. He was a rebel, and he found like-minded allies. In an interview with Lawrence Linderman, Carlin says, "The record of my life would show . . . a pattern of rebellion and of not completing things which required bowing down to authority" (*Gallery*, May 1973). Unlike Corpus Christi, Cardinal Hayes was too strict for the restless teenager. He wasn't about to bow down to anyone.

Carlin quit high school at age sixteen. He had eighteen months of secondary education when he left in 1953. He tried a couple of art schools but lost interest and skipped class regularly. He spent most of his time with friends. With no father laying down the rules, Carlin took to the streets as a teenager experiencing life unbounded and independent. As he told Linderman, "The guys I was tight with were very funny dudes. We had an extremely large number of people with quick wits and great verbal senses of humor . . . the days were filled with all kinds of adventures." Carlin valued these early friendships, some of which he kept for life.

Carlin had a strategy he named the "Danny Kaye Plan" after one of his favorite performers. In essence, it matched his answer years earlier to what he wanted to be when he grew up: a radio deejay, then a stand-up comic, and then the ultimate, an actor. The values he learned from Corpus Christi took. The future would take care of itself if you had a plan.

Carlin told Larry Wilde at Laugh.com in 2002, "I did things that gained approval, attention, applause, approbation: all these A's that I never got in school I got by acting out for people." After he quit high school, Carlin's mother began pushing him to pursue a straitlaced career, going to college and getting a job in advertising. She wanted him to conform to her vision of the ideal man, one that was conservative and respectful, unlike her former husband. Yet Mary also nurtured his individuality and encouraged him to make people laugh. Carlin was confused. "The pressure was unbearable," he admitted when Sam Merrill of *Playboy* magazine asked him why he often ran away from home. "She had it all worked out. 'You'll become one of those smart-looking fellows in their Madison Avenue suits' . . . I rebelled against her and her values and her plans for my future at every opportunity" (*Playboy*, January 1982).

By way of escape, with the consent of his mother, he enlisted in the U.S. Air Force in 1954 rather than waiting for the draft, which remained in effect despite the Korean War having ended the year before. His brother Patrick had recently finished his tour of duty, so it was a logical choice. Carlin's short-term aim was to complete his service, collect the GI Bill money, and go to deejay school to kickstart the Danny Kaye plan. Carlin's "street cunning" would serve him well in his early years as he found his own course, away from the clutches of his mother.

In 1975, on an episode of *The Mike Douglas Show* cohosted by George, Mary would finally concede that her thirty-eight-year-old son would never join the Mad Men club. She still preferred the clean-cut version of her boy in the nice suit and tie, whereas when Carlin changed his look, it initially shocked her that her son had grown a beard and longer hair. She recalled that first sighting to Douglas and told it in a style worthy of a seanchaí: "Not a word did I know," Mary told Mike with her son beside her. "He suddenly appeared in my home and there he stood. I went silent . . . and when I'm silent, there's trouble. So, he realized something was happening, and he said, 'Mother, don't you remember what you wrote in my autograph [book] when I finished Corpus Christi? . . . What did you say?' I said, 'George! Insist on being yourself always. In all ways.' He said, 'Mother! Eat your words!'" Her story had the audience howling. George reached over and kissed her on the cheek, looking embarrassed.

Mary Carlin would die in 1984 at age eighty-nine. Her passing had a profound impact on Carlin. In the *A&E Biography* portrait broadcast on April 12, 2000, his daughter Kelly says that her grandmother's death caused "a huge transformation in him. It was truly like a ton of bricks had been lifted off his shoulders. He was a changed man."

Years after her death, Carlin remembered her more affectionately. He told author and fellow comedian Judy Gold in 2001 that his mother "had aristocratic intentions," but she raised two sons during World War II, providing a stable home life during an unstable time in history.

For a guy who almost wasn't born, George Carlin's formative years were often sweet despite their challenges. Most important, he discovered his voice in a city that had millions of voices: New York.

Two

CARLIN IN NEW YORK

*I*n the northwestern section of Manhattan lies the Riverside Park wall. The wall follows the curve of Morningside Drive from West 120th Street to Riverside Park. Locals call it the "Question Mark" because of its shape. It's a place that represents the geographic and emotional epicenter of George Carlin, "the landscape that had shaped his soul" as his daughter so eloquently puts it in her memoir *A Carlin Home Companion* (2015).

What was it about this part of New York that helped form one of the most important comedians of the twentieth century? Diversity. No other city in America could've provided it. Carlin embodied New York's urban cultural attitude—an attitude and approach to life that was nurtured at a young age. As his daughter concludes, "He carried this neighborhood in his heart no matter where he was in the world."

George Carlin was born at a fascinating time in the history of New York City. By 1937, the Great Depression was well under way and would continue through to the onset of World War II. When the war ended in 1945, New York was the major beneficiary of African American migration from the rural South, along with an influx of immigrants from Puerto Rico. This trend took place over decades, as new immigrants filled neighborhoods and brought values and history that transformed New York's cultural landscape. Many of these working-class people wound up in Morningside Heights. The world had moved to Carlin.

Growing up in Morningside Heights, Carlin absorbed the diverse voices he heard. On *Occupation: Foole* (1973), Carlin's successful fourth album, he does a bit called "New York Voices." With perfect inflection, he mimics the speech patterns he heard on the street: a chorus of Puerto Ricans, Italians, Irish, and Black people. "I love that kind of purism, man, good street talk," says the comedian.

When he was seven years of age Carlin, his mom, and brother Patrick moved into a new apartment at 519 West 121st Street. Erected in 1926, the building is still there; it's a ten-story residence with "Miami" in gold script above the entrance. It's here that Carlin soaked up the culture, listening to the radio and reading his magazines. In the gatefold photos for *Class Clown*, his seminal third album, his street can be seen in the background. The photos reveal a playful kid posing for the camera in the comfort of his own block. In one picture, he's seen as a baby and in another as a five-year-old with a dog, mugging for the camera. We also see a picture with his friend Lefty and class photos of the kids who attended Corpus Christi school. In these photos, Carlin is happy, confident, and ready to put on a show. West 121st Street was his original stage.

In the acknowledgments to his second great book of humor, *Napalm & Silly Putty* (2001), Carlin pays special tribute to his "boyhood friends . . . who listened to my street-corner and hallway monologues when I was thirteen and gladdened my young heart by saying, 'Georgie, you're fuckin' crazy!'" It was his gracious nod to the first audience he entertained regularly on the well-worn streets of New York's Morningside Heights, a place he nicknamed "White Harlem."

In *Napalm & Silly Putty*, Carlin writes about his experience and what he learned from growing up in America's biggest city: "Living in New York is a character-builder; you must know who you are, what're you doing, where you're going and how to get there . . . New York people are tough and resilient." Anyone who has witnessed commuters using the New York subway system on a sizzling day in

August can attest to this. "Street cunning" was Carlin's phrase for it. "It may not be better ethically or morally," he told journalist Lawrence Linderman, "but for practical getting by and saving your own life in an emergency and knowing what to do in certain situations, at a given age you're just more sophisticated and more glib and everything like that if you're from the city" (*Gallery*, May 1973). The city's edgy cultural patchwork taught him how to be resourceful.

New York has given birth to a long list of buoyant comedians ranging from Larry David to Michael Rapaport and Whoopi Goldberg to Julia Louis-Dreyfus. New York comedians identify with the urban experience for many reasons, mainly because of the city's size and diversity, one of the best places in North America. It still serves as the refuge of the unwanted outsider looking for a home where they feel welcome. As far as ideas are concerned, the city acts like a huge organic garden seeded by sensitive artists. In Carlin's first book, *Brain Droppings* (1997), he writes that the 1995 World Series, in which the New York Yankees beat the Atlanta Braves in six games, was a class-versus-class matchup as "the gritty, tough, Third-World, streetwise New York culture triumphed over the soft, suburban, wholesome, white-Christian, tacky mall culture of Atlanta."

The urban vitality of New York fueled Carlin's early years. His friends at school provided an audience, principally on street corners in Morningside Heights where everybody thinks he's a comedian. But Carlin was special, and he worked the young crowd because the city—in fact, the very block at West 121st Street—gave him the creative freedom to be outrageous. As he notes in *Brain Droppings*, "New York is a large man saying, 'Fuck You!'" Carlin loved being that large man even though he only grew to be five foot nine. New York provided him with ideas, characters, and voices cut by a sharp-edged attitude.

Carlin had a rich bounty of influences on the rough-and-tumble streets of Morningside Heights. One block to the south of where he lived is Columbia University. One block north of Broadway is the Jewish Theological Seminary, established in 1886. Across the street from the seminary is the Manhattan School of Music at 130 Claremont Avenue, the main building of which backs onto Broadway. (The school's west side faces Grant's Tomb in Riverside Park.) On Broadway west of 121st Street lies the Union Theological Seminary, so vast that it occupies the full block. Across Claremont Avenue is Riverside Baptist Church. To the east, Carlin was within walking distance of the Apollo Theater in Harlem, separated by Morningside Park, home to ballyards and benches where he and his brother Patrick often smoked dope. This diverse weave of culture, academia, and religion made for interesting bedfellows in Carlin's mind.

One of his favorite places to go was the Nemo Theater at the corner of 110th Street and Broadway, a movie house erected in 1919. It would close in 1963, but in 1947, it was George Carlin's second home, site of a movie that would be another inspiration to him, *The Kid from Brooklyn*, starring Danny Kaye. Samuel Goldwyn produced the RKO picture, which was a musical-comedy remake of the Harold Lloyd picture *The Milky Way* (1936), about a milkman who becomes a boxing champion. The movie showcases Kaye's remarkable facial expressions and physicality. To a young, wide-eyed ten-year-old, it was comedy gold. A year later, Kaye starred in one of the biggest movies of his career, *The Secret Life of Walter Mitty*, based on the short story by James Thurber. Kaye's ability to play eight distinct characters, along with his performance of the lyrically masterful tune "Anatole of Paris," composed by Sylvia Fine, entranced Carlin.

When he was older, the center of Carlin's world would be Moylan's Tavern, a bar where many regulars became an extended family for George and his brother Patrick. Moylan's was in a great location. The bar, which closed in the mid-1970s, was on Broadway Avenue between La Salle Street and Tiemann Place. As a working-class saloon serving a broad ethnic mix of drinkers, Moylan's was the place where Carlin could relax, have a beer, shoot pool, and hear the latest news from the street. Carlin would eventually use it as the setting for his FOX-TV series in 1994.

In 1961, he took his fiancée, Brenda, to visit Moylan's. Brenda, a midwesterner, handled the scrutiny well, according to Carlin. Brenda was a hit, drinking at the bar alongside the men and generally matching the low-key, blue-collar vibe of the place. Endorsement from the patrons at Moylan's meant a lot to Carlin as a stamp of approval from people who mattered to him.

In his later years, Carlin would don one of several baseball caps featuring logos that summed up his relationship to New York. One had New York™ and the other LIVE HARD spelled out along the top. It was a simple way for Carlin to recall the memories of his childhood, the boys and girls he hung around with, and the adventures so indelibly etched into his impressionable mind.

In 2014, comedian Kevin Bartini led a group of lobbyists who worked with Councillor Mark Levine to rename West 121st Street "George Carlin Way," but it wasn't easy. The name change arrived despite the opposition of the Corpus Christi Catholic Church at number 529. Priests at the church were opposed to "George Carlin Way" according to Bartini, who told Jack Buehrer of the *Village Voice* (October 21, 2014) that "[they] the church . . . were trying to protect their students against dirty words." The parish leaders were afraid their pupils would use their computer savvy to discover Carlin's work and his commentary on religion, faith, and the church's messages. In the *Village Voice* story, Bartini says that criticism of the Catholic Church and its doctrine would be "bad for business." This was six years after Carlin died, and they still considered his ideas dangerous to students and parishioners!

But it was deeper than that, according to Pastor Raymond Rafferty, who had known Carlin as a boy. When the name change came to light, he told CBS News in 2011, "Carlin made a mockery of this particular place . . . he was also an extremely vulgar person." The old pastor could not let go of his own steadfast belief that Carlin was trouble from the get-go. (Ironically, Carlin himself often thanked the priests and nuns who were a big part of his upbringing. He even lists them on the jacket of *Class Clown*.) Clearly not familiar with his album and dedication, Pastor Rafferty evoked only one image, the snot-faced brat named Georgie. In the end, Rafferty was vindicated: "George Carlin Way" runs only to Amsterdam Avenue from Morningside Drive, short by one block from the church. After three years of debate, Mayor Bill de Blasio made the change official on October 22, 2014.

Carlin finally gets his way. From L to R, Kevin Bartini, Sally Wade, Patrick Carlin and Kelly Carlin-McCall. HOO-ME / SMG / ALAMY STOCK PHOTO

THREE

TWICE THE LAUGHS: BURNS AND CARLIN

In March 1960, George Carlin and his friend Jack Burns purchased a new Dodge Dart Pioneer with tinted windows and drove west to the land known for cement ponds and movie stars: Hollywood. They had fifteen minutes' worth of written material, $300, and all their possessions. With a full tank of gas, a six-pack, and a lot of positive energy, they set out to seek their fame and fortune in Tinseltown. Burns was twenty-six. Carlin was twenty-two.

They took the Dixie Overland Highway from Fort Worth, Texas, to El Paso, Texas, then straight to California through the desert. Today, it's known as U.S. Route 80. This was the road to stardom in the hearts and minds of Burns and Carlin. They were partners in comedy looking to make it big, joking to each other about being on television talk shows. Was it a shot in the dark? There was only one way to find out: pack up and go. So they quit their jobs and hit the road. The trip was almost dreamlike in intensity, a ramshackle odyssey of the kind that Jack Kerouac immortalized in *On the Road* just a few years earlier.

The path to Carlin and Burns's trip began after Carlin joined the air force in 1954. On completing basic training, he was stationed in Shreveport, Louisiana. There, he met Mike Stanley, who was an actor in a small theater group. Stanley was from Mississippi, and when he met Carlin, he took an instant liking to him. Carlin's energetic personality got him cast in his first play, *Golden Boy*, by Clifford Odets.

He played a trainer in act 1 and a photographer in act 2. Another man named Joe Monroe played the role of Tom Moody, manager of the lead character, Joe Bonaparte, a boxer who really wanted to be a musician.

Monroe was part owner of KJOE, a popular Top 40 radio station that played all the latest hits from the emerging stars of rock and roll, such as Elvis Presley. Carlin asked for a tour of the station and the chance to watch him to do his show. Monroe agreed and invited Carlin to read some copy by way of an audition. Carlin had an obvious New York accent, but Monroe hired him anyway to work as a newscaster on the weekends. For listeners in the South to hear a guy from the upper west side of New York City must have sounded a little weird but not to Monroe. Carlin, with the blessing of his commanding officer, who issued an off-base permit, got a regular show from noon to 3 p.m., Monday to Friday.

Carlin's career in radio was officially launched. But his service in the U.S. Air Force was full of the rebellious behavior that got him kicked out of school, only this time, it was the air force's turn. Carlin was court-martialed three times: once for deserting his guard duty post, a second time for insubordination, and finally a third time for too many Article 15 offenses. (These are minor offenses, such as smoking marijuana or being drunk while on duty.) Like his time in school, Carlin was pushing against authority. Here, it was the noncommissioned officers in the air force. After three years, they gave Carlin a discharge that still made it possible for him to get the benefits of the GI Bill. He continued to work as a deejay.

Carlin's few months at KJOE were invaluable. He worked on his game, lost his accent, and developed his personality as a radio guy. Joe Monroe gave him some latitude on air that led to his biggest shift: the afternoon drive slot from 2 p.m. to 6 p.m. weekdays. On the number one station in Shreveport, *Carlin's Corner* made him a star. He even got his own up-tempo theme song with a chorus of voices singing,

"It's time to smile and swing a while, with Carlin . . . the smoothest record man anywhere . . . get set to listen 'cause here we go on the George Carlin show!" This sixty-second nugget was made available on the 1999 Little David collection box set. The track reveals a twenty-year-old ex-serviceman comfortable in his own skin.

After the successful gig at KJOE, Carlin joined WEZE radio, Boston, in 1959. He was chief operator and host of a late-night program of middle-of-the-road pop music featuring Frank Sinatra, Vic Damone, and Rosemary Clooney. He took the job because it was in a larger market than Shreveport. (Ambitious deejays are inclined to work in bigger markets; Carlin was no exception.) As a broadcaster, the format wasn't an ideal situation for the former host of *Carlin's Corner*, who preferred rhythm and blues. WEZE was part of the NBC radio network in a news-oriented format. Music was filler in between spoken-word shows, including religious programming from Cardinal Cushing, close friend of the Kennedy family.

The news director was Jack Burns. Born in Boston in 1933, Burns had grown up under the shadow of his father, an officer in the U.S. Air Force. So when he came of age, Burns joined the U.S. Marines and served during the Korean War. They discharged Sergeant Burns in 1954 after his return home. He then enrolled in the Leland Powers School near Brookline, Massachusetts. Founded in 1904, the school focused on courses in theater, dance, and public speaking. The introduction to one early edition of the school's handbook reads, "If you have a word of good cheer, a thought of courage, a vision of the joy of life, the world is hungry to hear it." Burns couldn't resist the delightful invitation. He wanted to pursue acting. Failing that, a job in radio would be a steady alternative. If he couldn't get parts, his teachers believed, he could sharpen his delivery with public speaking courses.

After graduation, Burns signed up for classes in New York with the renowned actor and teacher Herbert Berghof, a charter member of the Actors Studio. Feeling that postwar creativity, Burns was inspired by the "method" actors of the day, such as Marlon Brando, who was himself a cofounder of the Actors Studio. He had a promising start; Robert Anderson cast Burns in an off-Broadway production of *Tea and Sympathy*, but he couldn't land any more roles after the play closed. So he left New York, returned home, and went into broadcasting full-time.

Burns got his first job at WEZE radio in Boston, sure enough, as a newsman. By the end of the decade, he had become news director, interviewing upcoming politicians such as John F. Kennedy and even traveling to Cuba to interview Fidel Castro in 1958. His most memorable conversations were with George Carlin. As a couple of Irish Catholic boys, they had a lot in common. They were ex-servicemen who enjoyed a glass of beer, sharing stories, and making jokes.

Burns was also a mentor. Carlin learned a lot about politics from him, seriously encountering left-wing ideas for the first time in his life. As he tells it in *Last Words*, it was through Burns that he began to appreciate that "the Right defends . . . property rights, while the Left fights for civil and human rights." It's hard to believe today, but Carlin had until this point leaned conservative and supported the Republican Party. His mother was a big supporter of Dwight D. Eisenhower and took the Red Scare tactics of Senator Joseph McCarthy seriously. Whereas Carlin never finished high school and didn't really know much about history, Jack Burns was an educated newsman with a social conscience. Carlin's respect for his friend's ideas and rationale left an impression on him. Their relationship was a potent blend of politics, culture, and comedy.

One weekend, Carlin took the station's news car to New York to score some weed, as he often did. The station wagon had "WEZE 1260, News of the Moment!" in bright lettering along the doors. Carlin drove to his old stomping grounds with a couple of mates who were also looking to score. After buying some weed in Harlem, Carlin dropped in to see his mother at her apartment in Morningside

Heights. The station manager in Boston tracked him down, called him there, and asked him to cover a story about a prison break at the Walpole penitentiary, about thirty miles southwest of Boston. Carlin brushed him off. When he returned to Boston, they dismissed him for abusing company property and not following orders. He had been there for about three months, always in conflict with authority figures as he had in his air force days. Being fired from a job he didn't really like carried the same weight as being court-martialed: it hurt but not too much.

While Burns continued to work in Boston, Carlin got a job at KXOL (1360 AM) in Fort Worth, Texas. Today, it's a Spanish-language Christian music station (KMNY), but in 1959, their format was Top 40 in one of the biggest radio markets in the United States. In May, they hired Carlin as their deejay from 7 to midnight, five nights a week, and gave him a lot of latitude. He tried voices and dialects and characters that became part of his show, including Al Sleet, the hippie-dippy weatherman. This was Carlin's dream job: he was earning $135 a week, playing records for the teens while they did their homework, answering the request line, and replying to fan letters, skills that would serve him well in the years ahead. In an interview with *Gallery* magazine in 1973, Carlin says, "It was the first time I recognized that honesty and candor on the air and off attracts people."

Meanwhile, Jack Burns—still hoping to make it big as a performer—quit WEZE and drove to Hollywood to pursue acting. He packed his old car and hit the road. When he stopped in Fort Worth to replace his worn-out tires, he hooked up with Carlin. Instead of continuing west, he took a job as the late-night newsman at KXOL, which had literally opened up the morning of his arrival. Burns and Carlin rented a two-bedroom apartment in the tony neighborhood of Monticello. In their spare time, they listened to comedy records by Jonathan Winters, Mort Sahl, Lenny Bruce, and Shelley Berman: four artists who distinguished themselves from the Vaudeville comics who came before them. Inspired, the roommates dreamed about appearing on the *Tonight Show* with Jack Paar. The partnership was on.

After working on some ideas, the duo tried their material in front of an audience. A local coffeehouse called the Cellar, so named for its dark and dingy interior, had a beatnik ambience with music, poetry readings, and comedy. Burns and Carlin took to the small stage a few times and improvised most of their act. It was rough and raunchy, but the crowd, often drunk on Everclear grain alcohol, loved it. Motivated, the pair worked hard to come up with something new for each performance. Out of those shows came good stuff that they would refine and incorporate into their professional act.

Burns and Carlin felt that satiric humor with an edge was the way to go, and they didn't have to look far for inspiration. Carlin told Larry Wilde in an interview on Laugh.com in 2002, "We felt connected to that movement that was starting then that Lenny Bruce and Mort Sahl had certainly been the best exponents of . . . coffeehouse comedy more than nightclub comedy." Nightclub comedy was basically telling jokes. Burns and Carlin had higher aspirations. They wanted to be a crossover act in tune with the new generation of comedians who emerged out of the 1950s, such as Mike Nichols and Elaine May, Shelley Berman, and Bob Newhart. Nichols, May, and Berman came out of Chicago's Compass Players, founded by Paul Sills and David Shepherd in 1955. They improvised a show where the "script" changed night after night. Four years later, Sills would cofound Second City with Bernard Sahlins and Howard Alk.

Bob Newhart's deadpan, stammering act was clever and satiric at the same time. His first album was *The Button-Down Mind of Bob Newhart*. Recorded in 1960, the record sold more than 600,000 copies on release. So there was a market for a new style of comedy that was smart and acerbic. Burns and Carlin knew they had to try it in Hollywood, where the clubs, the money, and the opportunity lay. Burns was headed in that direction anyway.

In February 1960, the pair quit their day jobs in Fort Worth and headed west with fifteen minutes of what they considered comedy gold propped up by a lot of hope. Their dream of making it big in California was one step closer. When they arrived, Burns and Carlin purchased new suits, checked into the local YMCA, and started looking for work as entertainers. They wouldn't settle for anything less. A month later, their money ran out. So the two of them auditioned for a morning show at KDAY, a 50,000-watt radio station in Redondo Beach, California. They were hired and renamed the Wright Brothers, literally doing a show from an airplane on their debut. They worked on their act each night after the station signed off at sundown.

Murray Becker, who used to be the road manager for the comedy duo Rowan and Martin, had his office in the same building as KDAY. One evening, he spotted Burns and Carlin working on their performance after hours. He liked what he heard. Becker became their biggest fan, stepped up to be their manager, and started dropping their names to anyone who mattered in Los Angeles. Becker's showbiz connections ran deep. He knew Mort Sahl's manager Milt Ebbins, and he knew Lenny Bruce from his days in the U.S. Navy. He also got them their first recording contract with Herb Newman's label, Era Records. Becker wasted no time promoting his newest act. Burns and Carlin had been in Hollywood for only six months.

With Becker's help, the duo was making money and filling coffeehouses with their fresh brand of humor. Their act included Carlin's impressions of Lenny Bruce and Mort Sahl. It was a risky choice to mimic two of the most popular fringe comedians, but to Carlin, it was as much a tribute as it was parody. One night, Bruce and his wife Honey caught their show at Cosmo Alley. He was flattered by Carlin's impression so much that he recommended they be signed by GAC, the talent agency that represented him.

After seeing their routine at Cosmo Alley, Mort Sahl recommended Burns and Carlin to Hugh Hefner, who had established

Playboy magazine and was now branching out with a chain of Playboy Clubs. Chicago was the site of the first one; it was a commercial hit with more than 100,000 members visiting the club by the end of its first year in business. As the number of clubs grew, Hefner provided entertainers with a venue in almost every major city from New York to Los Angeles. Hefner was a booster. One of his favorite comedians was Lenny Bruce, who not only played the club circuit but also was a regular guest on the publisher's short-lived syndicated *Playboy's Penthouse* TV show, which ran from 1959 to 1961. (Carlin appeared on the follow-up *Playboy After Dark* in 1970.) Hefner caught Burns and Carlin at the Cloister Inn on Rush Street in Chicago, steps away from his own club. Their cheeky routines impressed him, so he booked the duo into the Playboy Club.

By June, Burns and Carlin had a manager, an agent, and a recording deal. The motivation to keep writing, adding skits, and developing characters was now going to fuel their work for the next two years. With an aim to be as current as possible, their material took shots at the sincerity of charities and organized religion and poked fun at anticommunist groups, such as the John Birch Society. Carlin told Judy Stone of the *New York Times* about their approach: "We shared a similar attitude toward authority. We felt that a comedian should be more or less a spokesman for people against authority, and have certain attitudes toward The Establishment, bureaucracy and small-mindedness" (May 28, 1967). Burns and Carlin did topical humor that often crossed the line of poor taste, but they never used profanity because they considered their act "clean," and their reputation as a "clean act" got them work. Murray Becker expected no less.

Hefner went a step further too when Burns and Carlin made the pages of the January 1962 issue of *Playboy*. The article calls them "sicknik comedians," 1950s slang for comics who were cynical, satiric, and offensive. Over three pages, *Playboy* describes "their vivisection of the fatuous TV fare beamed at the kiddies" and lays out a transcript of "Captain Jack and Jolly George." The routine features two hosts suggesting to kids where to hide their booze and how to get a "junior junkie kit" featuring pure heroin, a bent spoon, and a 12-cc hypodermic needle. On paper, it's only half funny because it's missing the inflections and high-energy delivery heard in performance. Nevertheless, the pictures reveal how the two comics looked in front of an audience: presentable! In the fully clothed photo spread, Burns and Carlin make faces and duplicate moves typical of their live show.

The misnamed *At The Playboy Club Tonight* album is their only recorded performance just months after the team arrived in Hollywood. In fact, they taped it at Herb Cohen's Cosmo Alley in May 1960. Released on Era Records three years after the duo broke up, the album captures Burns and Carlin playing with great timing, commitment, and assurance. The LP has only seven tracks running about thirty-five minutes. Yet in that precious half hour, we hear the twenty-three-year-old George Carlin shaping his deejay persona and bringing into focus his early comedic style.

Two tracks stand out from this "bright new comedy team," as the emcee says at the opening, the previously mentioned "Captain Jack and Jolly George" and Carlin's solo bit titled "Mort Sahl/Lenny Bruce." The duo explodes with the first sketch featuring a couple of boisterous hosts of a children's show. No math or spelling lessons on this program: it's about safely taking heroin, selling your body on the street with instructions from Lolita (from the Nabokov novel), and consuming your "milk"—White Horse scotch whiskey. After all, this show is for the "hip kiddies" who take risks and get high.

In a slightly absurd non sequitur, Burns mentions a picture of Alexander King, who was a frequent guest on the *Tonight Show* with Jack Paar. King was a bit of an eccentric. Married three times, he was a morphine addict and the author of several books of humor. The idea of getting an eight-by-ten picture from this creepy Brit to hang on the bedroom wall proves the duo was going for edgier material.

Satirizing children's TV programming meant that they were taking shots at *Buffalo Bob*, *Romper Room*, and *Captain Kangaroo*, three of the most popular kids' shows in the 1960s. Burns and Carlin wrote this sketch to mock all the straitlaced programming aimed at children. To them, kids' shows were extended commercials disguised as educational media. The entire piece is absurd, subversive, and smart. Sickniks indeed.

Burns and Carlin knew they could challenge an audience linking literary culture with TV culture, combined with drug and alcohol abuse. Their humor is layered. Here are two young comics, making people laugh with a creative mix of high- and lowbrow ideas that are not, in their minds, mutually exclusive.

The album closes with George Carlin's impression of Bruce and Sahl. Here, for the first time, Carlin acknowledges, on record, his most important influence. Carlin had discovered Bruce on the album *Interviews of Our Times* (1958) when he was in Shreveport when his roommate Jack Walsh brought the record home. Years later, he told journalist Judy Stone, "Lenny's perception was magnificent. He could focus on the real emotions and motives behind what we say and what we do in our society. He was the immortal enemy of cant and hypocrisy and pseudo-liberalism, which is just another form of hypocrisy" (*New York Times*, May 28, 1967). Inspired yet overwhelmed by Bruce's genius even on record, Carlin worked on an impression of Lenny that he wrote into his stage act with Burns. It was his way of paying tribute to someone he admired as an artist. It's a first-rate Bruce imitation. He studied Bruce's sound, delivery, and pace. Carlin reproduces the "Djinni in the bottle" story from Bruce's debut album, and it's just as funny as the original: a note-perfect cover version.

Once again, he captures the warm baritone of Sahl perfectly. As Sahl, Carlin goes into an original monologue with a story about two college students in Japan who take a course in "rioting," poking fun at student activism. He closes the bit by giving the real reason President Eisenhower's trip to Japan was canceled: because they wanted to see General MacArthur and TV host Jack Paar walking in from the ocean together. Carlin was referencing a famous image of MacArthur walking in knee-deep water at the beachhead in Leyte, the Philippines, in 1944. What we hear on this record is no ordinary talent: ridiculous and downright crazy but, taken as a whole, the start of something bigger. The class clown was planting his own seeds for later harvest.

Burns and Carlin split up in March 1962. In their last routine, they convened, privately, in a suite at Chicago's Hotel Maryland. It was the location of their first notable appearance, five floors below, in the Cloister Inn, when they opened for jazz singer Bobby Short. In that pivotal last meeting, they divided their cash earnings, smoked weed, and drank to their achievements. Burns and Carlin had reached full circle and remained friends. The next night, Carlin was onstage at the Gate of Horn, another venue in the city. He was the third act in a night that featured folk singers Miriam Makeba and Peter, Paul and Mary.

The partnership had been a fruitful experience for both men. They performed all over America, including a free show at the Cellar in Fort Worth in 1961. But the real highlight was an appearance on the *Tonight Show* in October 1960, with guest host Arlene Francis. On their biggest TV appearance, they did six minutes in a bit featuring impressions of NBC journalists Chet Huntley (Burns) and David Brinkley (Carlin) and interviewing Richard Nixon (Burns) and John F. Kennedy (Carlin), one month before what was to be a very close election. As Carlin reflected on their quick rise to fame in a conversation with Jenni Matz in 2007, "1960 was five years telescoped into one" (Interviews.televisionacademy.com).

In Chicago, Burns started working and writing for the Compass Players. There, he met Avery Schreiber forming Burns & Schreiber, a clever new act leading to regular appearances on television and several albums. Burns pursued his dream of becoming an actor as well, getting to fill the shoes of Don Knotts for a season of the *Andy Griffith Show* as the bumbling deputy Warren Ferguson. His real claim to fame might be his faux fight with Andy Kaufman on ABC's *Fridays* on February 20, 1981. Burns was a producer on the comedy show, which rivaled *Saturday Night Live* (*SNL*) at the time. During a scene, he comes from behind the cameras and takes a couple of weak punches at Kaufman for throwing water in the face of Michael Richards, his costar, during another sketch. All three were in on the gag, but it broke the fourth wall unexpectedly. Looking at it again, forty years later, this precious TV moment doesn't have the same impact, but it reflects Burns's fearlessness as a comedian.

Even though their joint career lasted only about twenty-four months, it was rooted in the friendship of Burns and Carlin and their belief in each other's ability to make people laugh. When Carlin received his star on the Hollywood Walk of Fame in 1987, it was placed at the corner of Vine and Selma, steps away from their first job in radio. They were quite the team, gaining a broad audience in the "frontline clubs" like the Playboy in New York and Chicago, knowing they could succeed *together* doing comedy.

Yet Carlin knew he wanted to go solo as early as 1961 after he married Brenda Hosbrook. As he admits in his memoir, *Last Words*, he was reluctant to share his best material with Jack, describing himself as "selfish with my creativity." Jack Burns opened Carlin's mind, broadened his political perspective, and helped him reveal his own voice. Inspired by Mort Sahl's wordplay and Lenny Bruce's boldness, the class clown was going solo as a nonconformist, ready to become a full-time stand-up comedian.

Four

THE NONCONFORMISTS: MORT SAHL, LENNY BRUCE, AND RICHARD PRYOR

*I*n 1997, George Carlin celebrated forty years in show business with a Home Box Office (HBO) special. Jon Stewart, future host of the *Daily Show*, introduced him as a member of what he considered the "holy trinity of stand-up"; the other two were Lenny Bruce and Richard Pryor. Lenny Bruce, who died at age forty-one in 1966, is remembered today as a hero of stand-up, a man often deprived of his First Amendment rights, hurting for his art. Richard Pryor's remarkable style of transgressive comedy spoke truth to Black audiences while entertaining and enlightening White audiences. Considering the history of comedy, Stewart's biblical phrase seems appropriate. Carlin's inventive approach to stand-up reflected his observations during an era of cultural and political change beginning in the early 1970s. Yet the seeds of change from which he emerged germinated in the fertile ground of the post-war years.

The 1950s was in some ways the most artistically bold and expressive decade in the history of the United States up to that point. The sound track was jazz, dominated by bebop. In theater and motion pictures, method acting was emerging as an intense and realistic portrayal of American life. Julian Beck founded the Living Theatre, leaving the classics on the shelf by investing time with plays by Picasso, Pirandello, and Brecht. The so-called beat generation, led by poets Allen Ginsberg, Lawrence Ferlinghetti, and Jack Kerouac, was rejecting the old rules of writing and exploring sex, Eastern religion, and psychedelic drugs. Harvey Kurtzman launched *Mad* magazine in 1952 to satirize American culture. Hugh Hefner's *Playboy* debuted in 1953, an escapist magazine directed at men. Marlon Brando, James Dean, and others became role models for an entire generation of actors looking to express a deeper truth in their work, erasing the idealism of the previous generation.

The same held for the group of painters known as the abstract impressionists. Their notoriety was on full display in a famous photograph called "The Irascibles" published in *Life* magazine in 1951. It featured Jackson Pollock, Mark Rothko, and Willem de Kooning. The so-called late modern era in dance pioneered by Martha Graham also complemented these visuals and music changes. In 1958, the great Alvin Ailey started the first African American dance company in New York. Black writers such as James Baldwin and Alex Haley were breaking through to a wider audience along with the rise of the civil rights movement led by Martin Luther King Jr. No wonder there was room for something new in stand-up comedy.

Enter Mort Sahl.

In 1952, Sahl debuted as the first modern comic of the postwar era. When he launched his career in Los Angeles, he dispensed with typical joke telling characteristic of Vaudeville. He just *talked*. He didn't tell a joke and wait for a laugh in the customary Vaudeville style. His act was personal, cynical, and intellectual; he made people laugh with his clever blend of social commentary and satire. He pointed out the absurdities in the world, attracting a young, well-educated audience. Sahl's fresh, original style of comedy paved the way for comedians of all stripes, especially for Jon Stewart's "holy trinity of stand-up."

Sahl was born in Montreal, Quebec, in 1927. His father Harry was a closet playwright but had to settle instead for work as a customs clerk in Los Angeles. After a divorce in 1924, he placed a magazine ad for a friend with the question "Is there still a woman out there who would like to meet a dreamer?" And sure enough, there was, when Dorothy (Dora) Schwartz of Montreal responded to his bold question. According to biographer James Curtis in *Last Man Standing: Mort Sahl and the Birth of Modern Comedy* (2017), Dorothy made the trip to Los Angeles and had a roaring good time. She married Harry after three days of courtship.

Times were tough: Harry couldn't keep a steady job in Southern California, so he and his new bride moved to Montreal. His father-in-law, Benjamin Schwartz, supported them. Schwartz had clout. He was a Romanian refugee who settled in Quebec at the end of the nineteenth century and worked to become a successful buyer of real estate. He insisted on a European life in style and custom, including a traditional Shabbat meal each week. It was a meager start for Harry working in a cigar store on Bernard Avenue in neighboring Outremont, but he kept writing. After Mort was born, Harry and Dora moved into their own apartment doing well until the economic downturn of 1929 changed everything. The cigar store closed in 1931.

Harry took a job in Washington, D.C. It was the first of a series of relocations for his young family. Eventually, the Sahls settled outside Los Angeles, a few miles away from the downtown core full of movie houses, a library where Mort read books on military history while attending school. As an only child, Mort loved his independence. Like Carlin, Sahl was a product of his surroundings in his Westlake neighborhood. He snuck into movie theaters on his own, eating up the American celluloid culture and developing values about right and wrong. One of his favorite movies of the era was Frank Capra's classic political picture *Mr. Smith Goes to Washington* (1939) starring James Stewart and Jean Arthur.

When he met the age requirement in 1945, after World War II ended, Sahl joined the U.S. Army Air Corps. They assigned him to

Alaska as a flight engineer. His goal was the elite military college known as West Point, but he grew impatient with the enrollment process at the academy and took a different route. Sahl's time in the military was problematic. He hated conformity. He made the mistake of thinking his beloved 1942 motion picture *To the Shores of Tripoli* was the real thing. It was nothing like the real thing. So he started a newspaper called *Poop from the Group*, which made fun of the army and its officers that soon got him into trouble. Biographer James Curtis describes what happened next: "Sahl spent eighty-three consecutive days cleaning pots, shoveling coffee, and helping to feed 7,000 men." With no future in the service and West Point a mirage, he didn't reenlist after they discharged him.

Sahl returned home to Los Angeles in 1947. He was twenty-two, and thinking about his next move would take time. Sahl enrolled at Compton Junior College and worked on the campus newspaper. He continued to spend time in his favorite movie theaters, skipping class. When he was home, he and his mother used to tune in to popular radio commentators Henry Morgan and Herb Shriner. Shriner, who hosted *Herb Shriner Time* until 1949, a daily program on CBS, had just the right combination of wit and sarcasm that engaged Sahl every time he heard him. Shriner's use of language fascinated Sahl because the broadcaster's subversive humor was intellectual *and* accessible to smart young people like him. Born in Toledo, Ohio, Shriner later made the move to television, hosting a game show called *Two for the Money* on NBC. The media star's mix of philosophy and critical humor made a powerful impression on Sahl. After college, he enrolled at the University of Southern California, earning a degree in city management, but his first love was writing.

Indeed, Sahl considered himself a writer first and comedian second. He worked hard at developing an act that would somehow translate to the stage. By day, he wrote short stories, one-act plays, and the occasional movie script. By night, he hung around jazz clubs like the Crescendo in Los Angeles, where he befriended bandleader Stan Kenton, whose progressive jazz group drew him back to the club night after night. Sahl was smitten with Kenton's love of the power of music. He even drafted an oratorio for Kenton that inspired Capitol Records to release *New Concepts of Artistry in Rhythm* (1953). Kenton felt a similar kinship toward Sahl. In the liner notes to a performance recording on Kenton's label, Creative World, in 1970, he wrote, "Mort is the classic epitome of comedic talent. Like the Jazz musician, his material is always improvisational, a bit mind bending and always right on target."

In 1952, having endeared himself to the jazz community, Sahl worked the intermissions at Stan Kenton's concerts at the Palladium. It was a 4,000-seat venue that was receptive to his act, but it never got him very far. He played New York but generated no interest from the East Coast crowds or booking agents. On the advice of his first wife Susan Babior, Sahl tried a new club in San Francisco called the hungry i. There, in front of a smaller, younger audience, he took the stage for the first time in late December 1953. Enrico Banducci, owner and operator of the club, took a liking to the young comic and his acerbic presentation. It was Banducci who suggested that Sahl drop the suit and adopt what became his signature look: a white open-collared dress shirt, sweater, slacks, and loafers. It was transforming. Sahl found his look and his act, modeled after the college students who often attended his shows. A typical Mort Sahl show featured his satiric take on the news of the day. With a couple of folded newspapers under his arm, his performances were clean and free form. He entertained audiences using his rich knowledge of history blended with his wacky sense of humor.

In 1956, Sahl made his prime-time television debut on the *NBC Comedy Hour*, following an appearance on Steve Allen's *Tonight Show*, which aired, as it does today, at 11:30 p.m. They produced the variety show in Los Angeles, and it reached the biggest audience for Sahl, boosting his profile and resulting in more nightclub bookings. Sahl's engaging humor at the end of the Joseph McCarthy era was just the antidote to those fearful years led by the "actions of the junior senator from Wisconsin," as journalist Edward R. Murrow once said. Sahl did seven minutes on *Comedy Hour*. After being told for several years that his act was for "intellectuals" and not ready for prime time, Sahl proved the critics wrong.

At this time, Sahl was headlining at the hungry i in San Francisco, and he was getting gigs at the Crescendo Club on Sunset Strip in Los Angeles. It was at the Crescendo where he met Lenny Bruce in 1957. Bruce was engaged to play the club by its owner, Gene Norman, for a sixteen-week run—not bad for a new stand-up looking to take his New York point of view to the hipsters on the West Coast.

Bruce and Sahl were a couple of Jewish lads who had a lot in common: an interest in jazz, radio shows, and movies. James Curtis, in his biography of Mort Sahl, *Last Man Standing* (2017), describes their nuanced relationship: "Mort and Lenny became friends, but there was always an undercurrent of distrust between them." Despite that tension, the two often worked at the Crescendo Club in West Hollywood, which had two rooms: the premier room, named the Crescendo, and upstairs the smaller, Interlude room. One time, it featured both comedians during the same week. The Crescendo room was the larger venue, often featuring jazz groups besides comedians. (In 1965, it changed ownership and was turned into a music club and renamed the Trip, a major venue for upcoming acts in Los Angeles, such as the Mothers of Invention and the Doors.) Hollywood's biggest movie stars, politicians, and newspaper journalists were frequent patrons.

It was at the Crescendo where Mort Sahl was taking the lead with his unique brand of social commentary. Meanwhile, Lenny Bruce was making a name for himself as a new, wild, and unpredictable comedian. They weren't competitors, so they split the audience to a certain extent. Sahl was more inclined to use clean language rather than obscene. Bruce wasn't afraid to punctuate his routine with a curse word. Sahl's oeuvre was more about "a rescue mission for America" as identified by James Curtis. Sahl found success with his topical act, which was more political than Bruce's. Bruce was still an acquired taste.

Mort Sahl made his first official comedy album in 1958 called *The Future Lies Ahead*. It was released on Norman Granz's Verve label, known for its excellent jazz albums. Recorded in performance at the hungry i, Sahl's debut was a hit that brought him notoriety. He described his act in a conversation with John Chancellor for NBC's *Outlook* in 1957: "I don't talk about the news. I'm a victim of the news. And it's all rebellion. Rebellion against authority." What George Carlin heard in the voice of Mort Sahl was a bright guy challenging mainstream ideas by digging deep into their meaning and

Mort Sahl during his heyday in the early sixties.
PHOTOFEST

getting laughs. It drew him to Sahl's conclusions about the absurdity of America's politicians, which made him laugh and think at the same time. Sahl was "an equal opportunity offender," to quote Frank Zappa. He took shots at conservatives and liberals. Carlin liked Sahl's act for his delivery and wordplay; he never cursed or embarrassed his audience, either. His art was on a higher plane, satirical wit fueled by anger and cynicism. As reported by Curtis in his biography, Sahl assessed his own act in these words: "nothing I say is factual; only truthful."

In 1960, Mort Sahl was the most popular comedian of the day. He was thirty-three. In August, he made the cover of *Time* magazine, and he was profiled in *The New Yorker* the same month. His popularity hinged on a vast upgrade from conventional joke tellers like Bob Hope. He appealed to college students, writers, and liberal thinkers. Over time, his act improved. His delivery became nuanced with inflections inspired by jazz, streams of consciousness that ebbed and flowed like a soloist, modeled after his close friend Paul Desmond of the Dave Brubeck Quartet, one of the biggest groups on the college and club circuit. Often, the band and Mort Sahl were on the same bill, the latter filling the intermissions with his unique perspective on the world.

Woody Allen caught his act at the Blue Angel club in New York when he was eighteen; he, too, was impressed by Sahl's skillful presentation that for him "changed the face of an art form." Sahl was the catalyst in Allen's decision to do stand-up in 1961. In his autobiography *Apropos of Nothing* (2020), Allen further explores the impact of Mort Sahl. "Mort was a genius who did a lot of political humor, which really had not been done as well before, and a million lesser talents figured they could do political humor, too. While a few could, most failed. One difference was between a comic choosing the political route and Mort being a genuinely informed, articulate, political person. But finally, it was that Mort had a dazzling personality, and the others did not. He was gifted hugely as a performer. So much so that other comedians didn't give him credit for performing, but said denigratingly, 'He just comes out and talks. And anyone can do that.' So, while others might do political jokes, even some very good ones, the audience was locking in to Mort's personality."

By the late 1960s, Sahl was enduring an uneven career. After going public with his support of Jim Garrison, the New Orleans attorney who questioned the Warren Commission report on the death of President Kennedy, his phone stopped ringing. His bookings for clubs and TV show appearances fell as quickly as his revenue. Sahl drifted in and out of fashion well into the 1970s, but he never quit. He hosted radio shows and short-lived talk shows with the occasional guest spot on the *Steve Allen Show* or *Dick Cavett*. In 1996, he released an audiobook called *Mort Sahl's America*, an entertaining look at the follies of liberal politics.

George Carlin attended the *All-Star Sahl-ute* marking the eightieth birthday of Mort Sahl in June 2007 at the Wadsworth Theater on the campus of the University of California, Los Angeles. The event featured a who's who of stand-up comedians, including Jay Leno, Albert Brooks, Harry Shearer, Jonathan Winters, and Shelley Berman, the last two being veterans of the postwar, original comics inspired by Sahl. After the event, Carlin helped Sahl by cutting him a check to cover some of his debts, according to author James Sullivan.

On October 26, 2021, Mort Sahl died at age ninety-four. He was at home, in a retirement complex in Mill Valley, California, just north of San Francisco. He had moved there in 2009 to seek what he called "political asylum."

*

The second key influence on Carlin was Lenny Bruce, born Leonard Alfred Schneider on October 13, 1925, in Mineola, New York, a small town on Long Island. His father Mickey immigrated to the United States from the United Kingdom in 1905. His mother was Sadie Kitchenberg, who was best known by her stage name, Sally Marr. She was a dancer, stagestruck when she was young after seeing the dashing Italian actor Rudolf Valentino during his very successful years in the silent movie era. Mickey was kind, supportive, and generous but emotionally unavailable, sending weird messages to his son about life: a mix of guilt, pity, and fears. Lenny found solace by listening to the popular kids' radio show *The Lone Ranger* on the Mutual Broadcasting System. After Lenny's parents divorced, his dad married Dorothy Cohen, and Lenny lived with them until he was seventeen on their Long Island home in Lawrence, New York. He had his own room, a set of encyclopedias (his father encouraged him to read), and a jukebox in the basement.

Sally Marr was an important part of Lenny's life, even though working in show business was more important to her than being a parent. Marr visited her son at her convenience, often taking him to unconventional places as a teen. One time, on his fourteenth birthday, Sally treated Lenny to a burlesque show in New York. She introduced him to a world of misfits featuring strippers, singers, and comedians that appealed to the impressionable youth. (George Carlin's mother Mary was an important part of his life too, but she never took him to a nightclub on his birthday. He snuck into those places on his own.)

Sally was an inspiring force in her son's life but less than a parent and more like a friend and colleague. In 1942, when Lenny settled in with his dad, she pursued her own artistic goals. Her act was a mix of bawdy humor, singing, and dancing in New York burlesque houses and wartime hot spots like Club 78. But it wasn't enough. Marr struggled after her divorce, often taking any job that came along to pay the rent. Lenny had a working father and stepmother, so he did okay as a teen.

Bruce joined the U.S. Navy on October 19, 1942, at seventeen, the same day his father enlisted in the army. His courses at Wellington

C. Mepham High School no longer engaged him, so he quit. He served two years aboard a cruiser, the USS *Brooklyn*, and saw action in the Italy offensive that combined Canadian, British, and American forces against the German and Italian armies. He steeped himself in the culture of the navy: tattoos, gambling, and locker-room jokes. In fact, Bruce's outgoing personality lent a kind of crazy relief to the stress that he and his mates endured. Like Mort Sahl, Bruce hated the authority figures he had to report to, and after the war, the navy discharged him for feigning homosexuality, an admission the doctors believed. Bruce understood how he could buck the system. They issued him an honorable discharge, according to Lennybruce .org, "by reason of unsuitability for the naval service." It's not known if Bruce showed up for his hearing in uniform or dressed as a dandy.

Bruce returned to New York when the Big Apple was emerging as the entertainment capital of the United States. During the next two years, he pursued show business as an actor and comedian, officially changing his name and going pro in 1947. When bookings were slow to come, Lenny spent his time with his fellow unemployed comics in New York's finest diners, such as Hanson's or Lindy's or the LaSalle cafeteria. These local hubs, where you could get a cheap meal, were the incubators for a new generation of comics. It's where jokes and stories were road tested among the patrons.

Bruce started his stand-up career as an impressionist. Like so many comics looking for work in show business, it was a safe and acceptable artistic choice. Bruce's act included an early, subversive bit called "The Bavarian Mimic." His routine featured the voices of James Cagney, Humphrey Bogart, and Edward G. Robinson, whose gangster pictures in the 1930s made them big stars. The Bruce twist was that all three characters had a heavy German-accented kind of English that only an excellent mimic like Bruce could provide. He carried a box of props, wigs, and hats, often improvising onstage besides his prepared material.

Bruce pressed on, but he grew tired of his own act. He wanted to change the picture and refocus his efforts by tapping into his own life for stories and experiences. Like Richard Pryor, who was nurtured by a bright and supportive teacher in Juliette Whittaker, Lenny Bruce was the disciple of one Joe Ancis. Biographer Albert Goldman says he was an extremely funny man, "the original sick comic," in *Ladies and Gentlemen, Lenny Bruce!* (1974). Ancis was a good friend of Rodney Dangerfield, but he never did stand-up; he entertained the struggling comedians who met for coffee at the local eateries, such as B & G or Hanson's, in New York. Ancis personified the sick humor delivery, which is best described by the Yiddish word "shpritz," meaning "spray" or "in your face."

Today, we use the word "caustic" to describe a performance that was called "sick" in the 1950s. One of the best at caustic humor was the late Sam Kinison, whose extraordinary delivery often climaxed with a loud, high-pitched scream. Kinison was a former preacher, so he knew how to voice a punch line.

Bruce refined "shpritz" over a long tutelage with Ancis, who still lived at home well into his thirties. During these formative years, Bruce's trademark stand-up style was taking shape. He was getting better at breaking down barriers of class, race, and gender, being funny while making a point. Bruce, like Mort Sahl, loved jazz and borrowed musical patterns from Charlie Parker and Thelonious Monk, the founders of bebop. He also loved their improvisations, entranced by "a non-scripted sense of self-discovery," as scholar Barry Sanders called it, taking place onstage. In the music that Mort Sahl held dear, Bruce followed the tempo and phrasing that he could easily adapt to form the sound of his delivery. He would speak quickly and quietly, slow and loud, or repeat a word for emphasis. Bruce shaped the English language any way he wanted.

Show business for Joe Ancis was fantasy. For Lenny Bruce, it was reality, a chance to act out his restless life, often under the influence

Lenny Bruce makes a point. PHOTOFEST

of a growing addiction to hard drugs. Bruce's goal was to blend intellectualism into his work, aiming higher from the traditional joke tellers of Vaudeville. His act included a poetic mix of philosophy and satire while touching on taboo subjects, such as religion. Like the sound of his mentor, Joe Ancis, Bruce was unrelenting. It was his way of overcoming his inherent fear of rejection, the most painful dagger to the heart of any stand-up comedian. As a mimic, the audience could take it or leave it. Albert Goldman reports that Bruce admitted to Joe Ancis in 1959 that "he was doing him," about which his teacher had no qualms: "Man, you're doing it and I'm not doing it . . . you're using it to make a social comment." Bruce's genius was his ability to take raw ingredients (politics, race, sex, and censorship) from the changing American society and make linguistic art. His unique talent to refine revise and hammer out his material into something fresh and off the beaten path distinguished him from the rest of Borscht Belt joke tellers of the era. Bruce took risks and got some gigs, and by 1955, people were taking notice.

In 1958, a young David Steinberg saw Bruce for the first time at the Gate of Horn in Chicago, and his life was changed. The comedian's demeanor, his hip clothes, and the way he walked the stage doing his act had a profound impact on the sixteen-year-old Canadian. In his autobiography *Inside Comedy* (2021), Steinberg describes what it meant to him: "[Bruce] was a revelation because he wasn't trying to be funny all the time. He was into the story, the way the character talked. Doing comedy is being smart, which I saw with Lenny. I suddenly knew that I wanted to be smart as much as I wanted to be funny. And then I realized that being funny is a version of being smart."

As the new decade unfolded, Lenny Bruce was gaining a larger following. Fans went to his shows, listening and laughing. He was taking more risks, especially with the English language. One of his new bits was called "*To* is a preposition; *come* is a verb." He based it on what people might say during sexual intercourse, liberating the phrase from the bedrooms of the nation. His gigs at strip clubs provided the right audience to road test his edgy commentary because you still have to get laughs as a stand-up comedian and the audiences were very tough in those places. So Bruce upped the ante and went "blue." It was a strategic choice and a creative one, as Albert Goldman points out in his biography of the comedian: "He always had to show his emotions, disclose his attitude and punish everybody he felt was accountable for his predicament . . . he began to define a special role for himself as a comedian." That role included the selective use of the English language and how the meaning of words could shift and be shaped by the user. He tossed away the wigs and hats of his early act and used his voice to express his truth. As writer and academic Barry Sanders said of Bruce, "He leaned heavily on the First Amendment stating, 'If I can't say 'Fuck You,' I can't say 'Fuck the government'" (*The Subversive Humor of Lenny Bruce* [2009]). As his language became coarser, he risked breaking state obscenity laws. In February 1961, Bruce got the ultimate gig: Carnegie Hall. He put on a great show, but the cops left him alone. The severe snowstorm that hit New York that night was probably a deterrent.

On October 4, 1961, police arrested Bruce for using the word "cocksucker" onstage at the Jazz Workshop in San Francisco. After a long trial, often with Bruce in a sorry state of health because of his drug addiction, he appealed. A jury of his peers found him not guilty of breaking California's obscenity laws. The negative publicity and media attention he attracted put him under a spotlight by police. They watched him everywhere he went, so much so that Bruce often kept his overcoat on during performances so that he could leave with the peace officers, as he called them, on demand. As Albert Goldman points out, "He felt a great craving for basic truths. . . . He wanted to personalize his act. He wanted to make his act himself."

Bruce continually found resistance from club managers worried about losing their liquor licenses if they booked him. For Bruce, the long, hard battle to maintain his "inalienable right" to free speech was becoming stressful. In February 1963, the state of California tried him for obscenity following performances at two clubs: the Troubadour and the Unicorn in Los Angeles. The trial was brutal. Bruce's mental and physical health suffered. Even though it ended in a mistrial, he still had to face the music in Chicago for obscenity at the Gate of Horn club the year before. In the Illinois courtroom, he represented himself and defended his right to free speech. But he didn't finish the trial after his arrest on February 23, 1963, for narcotics possession in Los Angeles. Sharp as he was—and he studied hard for the trial—he was found guilty, sentenced to one year in jail, and fined $1,000. In April, on appeal, the Illinois court freed him on a bail bond. He headed back to California and the safer confines of his house in Hollywood Hills, only to reappear in New York to face more police scrutiny.

Police arrested Bruce for obscenity in April 1964 at the Café Au Go Go along with owner Howard Solomon. Their trial lasted six weeks and was very popular with some artists, such as Bob Dylan and Elizabeth Taylor. Their petition of defense made little impact. Bruce was sentenced to four months in a workhouse on December 21, 1964. (On appeal, he was set free on bail and would die before the appeal hearing could ever take place. His conviction was never overturned, but thirty-seven years later, in 2003, Governor George Pataki pardoned Bruce—the first posthumous pardon in the history of New York State.)

By 1965, despite the work of his dedicated attorney, Harry Kalven, Bruce was becoming emotionally and financially exhausted from his ordeals. His act, if you could call it that, was reading the trial transcripts. Audiences failed to find the humor and eventually abandoned his shows. His income, even when he got the occasional booking, dropped. Bruce's descent into a steady diet of Methedrine, bennies, weed, and brandy became constant. He was obsessed with the legal fight, but he couldn't keep it up financially, dismissing his lawyers and declaring bankruptcy in October of that year. His last performance was at the Fillmore West in San Francisco in June 1966. The opening act was the Mothers of Invention, whose leader, Frank Zappa, asked Bruce to sign his draft card. Lenny declined.

Lenny Bruce's miserable end came on August 3 when he was found at home, naked on the floor of his upper bathroom. He was dead from what the coroner reported as "acute morphine poisoning," adding that "it is obvious the deceased was administering a narcotics injection but did not intend to kill himself." In his book, cowritten with Lawrence Schiller, Albert Goldman suggests that the conclusion of the coroner deflected any further investigation into Bruce's death. Had the Los Angeles authorities done so, Goldman, whose book many people consider the definitive authority on the life and times of Lenny Bruce, thinks the conclusion would have been much more ambiguous. He writes, "You find yourself wondering whether there is really an authentic distinction in a case like this between accidental and suicidal death . . . Lenny Bruce was lying on the narrow crack that divides the living from the dead. He was only marginally alive, and he was facing the end." Nevertheless, Lenny Bruce sealed his fate as an artist who truly suffered for his craft. Perhaps Bob Dylan said it best on his 1981 album *Shot of Love* when he sings, "Lenny Bruce was bad, he was the brother you never had."

When the world learned about the death of Lenny Bruce, comedy lost a soul mate but gained a savior, the "Jesus Christ of the First Amendment" in the words of Judy Gold, whose book *Yes, I Can Say That* (2020) is a well-written salute to freedom of speech. From her keen insight as a comedian, she writes, "[Bruce] died for our sins, or at least took a lot of the punches, stabs and bullets. . . . He made people uncomfortable because he exposed all their bullshit . . . using truth and humor."

*

Finally, Richard Pryor, the third member of the "trinity," born in Peoria, Illinois, on December 1, 1940. His grandmother, Marie Carter Bryant, who stood six feet tall, weighed 200 pounds, and wore size 12 shoes, raised him in a brothel after his parents' divorce in 1945. An intimidating woman in a business that needed one, she often packed a straight razor to protect her "employees." She operated two whorehouses and a nightclub in a town known as the Sin City of the Midwest, whose best customers included sailors and soldiers in the U.S. military. As Scott Saul states in the prologue to his excellent book *Becoming Richard Pryor* (2015), "The instabilities of his [Pryor] childhood—the confusion of love and violence—shaped him into the kind of person who is never at home with peace."

Pryor's home was full of emotional confusion. His parents, Buck Pryor and Gertrude Thomas Pryor, a former prostitute, divorced when Richard was five years old. As a child, Pryor often witnessed scenes of violence between them. As Saul derives in his biography of Pryor, "This was love in the spirit of the blues—crazy love, love as damnation, love as possession by devils, with little tenderness to act as a countervailing force." In 1946, once divorced, Gertrude moved to Springfield, Illinois, while Buck, the enforcer who won custody of his son, stayed in Peoria.

The dangerous environment of Richard Pryor's youth stood in steep contrast to George Carlin's. He was the only Black student in school and lived in fear of being found out that he lived on the worst side of town. It took many years for Pryor to emerge into the extraordinary comedian/actor we know today. His grandmother, whom he called "Mama," was the most influential person in his life: she took care of him with clean clothes, regular meals, and church on Sundays. She wasn't perfect, but Pryor's grandmother taught him how to behave with dignity and respect. Years later, he revealed a painful secret. An older boy sexually abused him when he was seven.

Pryor lived in fear of his father, who hit him when he got out of line. If the young Richard violated any restrictions as set out by his dad, such as a curfew, he was beaten. He wasn't a freewheeling kid on the street like George Carlin, who was encouraged by his mother and brother to find his own way in the world. Pryor's youth was much more unpredictable. Yet he found consolation in the movie houses of Peoria, becoming a fan of the B-movie westerns of the 1940s featuring Lash LaRue, who was a skilled user of the bullwhip. Many of the pictures opened with Warner Bros. cartoons that Pryor could identify with since his life was one that included loners and victims, according to biographer Scott Saul.

As a kid, Richard Pryor was adaptable. He could talk himself out of anything, especially if he got in trouble in school. At thirteen, his eighth-grade teacher, Mrs. Margaret Yingst, noticed his talent for clever delivery. She found him entertaining and gave the young boy a chance to make his classmates laugh every Friday afternoon for ten minutes. It was a long way from Pryor's *Live in Concert* movie from 1979, yet it was his start as a comedian. Another woman who boosted his self-confidence was Juliette Whittaker.

Nurture versus nature—can one person change the life of another? For George Carlin and Lenny Bruce, the answer was yes. For Richard Pryor, whose harrowing separation from his mother plagued him for the rest of his life, it was Juliette Whittaker, a professional theater director and producer. Pryor showed up at her door in 1955 when she was running a workshop called Juliette's Youth Theater Guild in Peoria. She was an artist who recognized Pryor's special but raw talents as an actor and comedian. But he lacked confidence. She took him seriously by casting him in plays and encouraging him to take creative chances. One of Pryor's earliest routines came out of this fertile time; he called it "Rumpelstiltskin." Whittaker provided the safe and supportive environment that helped Pryor grow as an artist, one that was lacking at home. It was also the place where the local

Black youth could socialize among themselves without experiencing the inherent racism of Chicago, some 170 miles to the northeast.

Unfortunately, Pryor lacked the discipline needed to apply himself to the art of comedy. Sure, he could make people laugh as a restless teenager, but he couldn't stay in school. By the time he was fourteen, he had enrolled and been expelled six times. When he registered in desegregated Central High, he was one of nine Black students. He struggled there, too. Once, in a fit, he punched a teacher and was expelled, never to return. At fifteen, Richard Pryor, like many Black kids his age, never finished his high school education. Over the next three years, Pryor worked the few jobs for which he was qualified: janitor or shoeshine boy, the latter at the prestigious Hotel Père Marquette in downtown Peoria.

In 1959, escaping from the constant turmoil at home and perhaps looking to straighten out his life, Pryor enlisted in the U.S. Army. It may have appeared to be the right choice—steady money, learn a trade, and perhaps build a new life—but it wasn't. After eighteen months, while stationed in Germany, they discharged him for stabbing a White soldier, by accident, in a feeble attempt at breaking up a fight. Despite the hardship and systemic racism he encountered in the army, Pryor persevered as he matured. This was in the summer of 1960, the year John F. Kennedy was elected president of the United States and Martin Luther King Jr. was gaining popularity in the civil rights movement. Pryor had reason for hope.

Returning home to Peoria after his terrible stint in the army, Pryor mulled around with little money, hanging out with streetwise gamblers and other assorted characters. He could make people laugh with his commentary about life in the neighborhood, and with little else going for him, he became the street-corner philosopher. He absorbed the stories from the local gentry, including Preacher Brown, a transient drifter who later became part of Pryor's characterizations, better known as the "wino." As Scott Saul writes in his book *Becoming Richard Pryor*, "In Preacher Brown, Richard found a riveting companion . . . who put no demands on him." Pryor soon discovered his comedic voice through characterization. It was a revelation for the twenty-year-old to channel his inner pain while satisfying his need to perform.

Pryor's old neighbor Harold Parker fulfilled his need for a stage. Peoria's nightclub scene was a strong one in the late 1950s, and Harold's Club, as it was called, was one of the most fancified in town. It was also a drug den of sorts, with plenty of marijuana and amphetamines for sale if you knew the right people. They named it after its fancy owner, Harold Parker, an outgoing, well-groomed man. He was described in 1959 as "the boy-wonder of Peoria" by the *Chicago Defender*, one of the most influential African American newspapers of its time, established in 1905. Pryor knew Parker, and one day, he walked into the club and asked for a job. He said he could play some piano and sing a few songs à la Nat King Cole. Parker gave him a chance, and Pryor's stage presence and courage, if not his performance, impressed him. Parker offered him a gig as bartender and performer during the intermissions. It wasn't much, but it launched Richard Pryor, a professional entertainer, because he had the freedom to come up with anything to fill that precious fifteen-minute slot nightly. According to Scott Saul, Pryor took full advantage of the opportunity: "Richard had his own body of material—the people he'd observed in Peoria's pulpits . . . and his comedy inclined to the off kilter and the zany."

Harold's Club closed in the spring of 1962 after the authorities busted Parker for bribing a police officer. Pryor moved on to another successful club called Collins Corner, whose all-Black audience was much more open to his brand of entertainment. Pryor loosened up and became more physical in his act. His dream job was to perform on television, specifically the *Ed Sullivan Show* in New York. And so, encouraged by his mentor Juliette Whittaker, Pryor set out for New York City before the year ended to road test his act.

The Chitlin' Circuit was the mainstay for most Black performers for the better part of the twentieth century. It comprised a network of venues from Atlanta to Washington, D.C., with stops in Chicago, Detroit, and Philadelphia. The final, most prestigious venue was the Apollo Theater in Harlem, site of so many debut performances, including Ella Fitzgerald, James Brown, and ex-Fugee Lauryn Hill. In fact, when Richard Pryor started his journey on the circuit in the fall of 1962, Brown recorded his breakthrough album, *Live at the Apollo*, in October. It spent sixty-six weeks on the Billboard Pop Album chart after its release in May 1963. It was a rite of passage for a Black artist to perform at the Apollo in front of a Black audience—if you could make it there.

By 1963, Pryor's challenges included a lack of gigs and a growing dependency on cocaine. But his chief obstacle was Bill Cosby, the most popular Black comedian in America. Cosby had just emerged from a successful run in Greenwich Village and made *Newsweek* magazine in a profile that money couldn't buy. The piece was subtitled *Humor for Everyman*, published on June 17, and it included Cosby's routine about a conversation between God and Noah. (The revelations about Cosby's reprehensible behavior with women lay far in the future.) Cosby was sucking up the money, the gigs, and the attention, and that made Pryor angry. So after a couple of gigs in Toronto, having read a copy of the *Newsweek* profile in Canada, he headed to New York to see if he could walk through the door that Bill Cosby had opened for Black comics. If Cosby was hot, maybe there was a place for him, too.

Pryor went directly to Harlem to pick up the Black urban vibe he needed to get crazy and talk. He had to be patient. He didn't get to play the Apollo because nobody knew him, so he went downtown and performed at Café Wha? and the Bitter End in Greenwich Village. Pryor

Richard Pryor, age 23, on stage at the Café Au Go Go in Greenwich Village.
PHILLIP HARRINGTON / ALAMY STOCK PHOTO

wound up at the Improv coffeehouse, where he befriended Henry Jaglom. Jaglom, who occasionally dropped acid, encouraged him to do improv to unleash his comedic soul. It was good advice. Pryor found instant gratification from the audience, performing unfiltered and wrapping himself in painful memories of his tormented life. It didn't pay the bills or his drug habit, so Pryor did *his* version of Bill Cosby. As Scott Saul points out in his book *Becoming Richard Pryor*, he studied Cosby's act and mimicked the comedian's style, "the rhythms, the make-believe scenario, the wacky, absurdist ending" that were features of Cosby's routines. It worked, and by March 1964, Pryor was getting gigs and growing his audience.

Pryor made his television debut in 1964 on a variety show called *On Broadway Tonight*, hosted by Rudy Vallée, performing as a confident yet twisted version of Bill Cosby. He failed to make a big splash. He continued to work the clubs in New York under the management and support of Manny Roth, who believed in him. Roth and Pryor worked new material into his act while polishing his delivery, his wardrobe, and his routine. Over time, he became less like Cosby and a little more like himself: a mix of physical comedy and self-deprecating humor.

In May 1965, Pryor got his big break on the *Ed Sullivan Show*, leading to regular appearances on the *Merv Griffin Show*, which had just gone into syndication. Pryor was now reaching millions of viewers. You can see most of these early appearances on YouTube.

Pryor finally got to play the Apollo Theater in August 1965. He wasn't rebooked for another six months. He returned with Redd Foxx, the de rigueur comedian in Black nightclubs long before playing the grumpy lead character Fred Sanford in *Sanford & Son* in 1972. Pryor spent some quality time under Foxx's tutelage in 1965 looking to cross over into movies or a regular TV series like Cosby's *I Spy*.

By the end of the 1960s, Pryor embraced Black culture from his singular perspective and channeled it into his routine. Biographer

Scott Saul writes, "His hurtling journey toward success was turning into a hurtling journey to find himself" (*Becoming Richard Pryor*). Eventually, he did. Pryor became a serious crossover artist, starring in major motion pictures, including *Car Wash* (featuring Carlin), *Silver Streak* (featuring Gene Wilder), the autobiographical drama *Jo Jo Dancer, Your Life Is Calling*, and the Billie Holiday biopic *Lady Sings the Blues*. He was nominated for ten Grammy Awards for Best Comedy Album, winning five, and he was the first recipient of the Mark Twain Prize for American Humor in 1998. Following a career that was in constant and creative motion, Pryor died in 2005 of multiple sclerosis.

*

In the spring of 1962, George Carlin began his journey as a solo stand-up comedian. He played as many one-nighters as he could, using Chicago as his base of operations. His wife Brenda joined him on this major leap of faith. During the next two years, Carlin worked on his act, wrote voraciously, and smoked an awful lot of weed, earning a living through it all. He built on the ideas he established with Jack Burns, including his killer impression of Kennedy. His look was the same: nice tie, nice suit, and no beard.

After Steve Allen left the *Tonight Show* to do his syndicated variety show in Los Angeles, Mort Sahl was hired to host for a week, four months before Johnny Carson took the job on October 1—one of many hosts, including crooner Pat Boone, actress Zsa Zsa Gabor, and TV personality Art Linkletter, to fill in at that time. His eclectic guest list included film director Otto Preminger, musician and friend Dave Brubeck, and a new stand-up comedian by the name of Woody Allen. And in June 1962, Sahl gave Carlin a five-minute spot on the *Tonight Show*, his TV debut as a solo act.

In December, they arrested Lenny Bruce on obscenity charges at the Gate of Horn club in Chicago, but he wasn't alone. George Carlin caught his show and witnessed the bust firsthand. When the police asked a drunken Carlin for ID, he said he didn't have it. Annoyed, they arrested him. The pair wound up in a paddy wagon and were hauled off to jail. The effect on Carlin was revolutionary. He was experiencing Lenny's life under the watchful eye of the police. Over time, Carlin reached an important conclusion that Bruce wasn't being arrested for obscenity; he was being arrested for making jokes about the Catholic Church. (In those days, a majority of police were Irish Catholics.) Carlin told Larry Wilde in an interview on Laugh.com in 2002 that "he [Bruce] was the first one to make language an issue and he suffered for it; I was the first one to make language an issue and succeed from it." But in 1962, Carlin was still doing his jester routine. He was ten years away from "Seven Words You Can Never Say on Television."

Years later, in 1966, George and Brenda Carlin would take a drive from their new home in Beverly Glen, California, to the Hollywood Hills to visit their old friend Lenny Bruce. He was holed up in his last refuge, licking his wounds from several hard-fought legal battles and standing up for his First Amendment rights. He was bereft of hope and trying to find solace by self-medicating with alcohol and drugs.

The visit was short but affectionate. Carlin said Bruce was as "lovable as ever" and in good spirits despite a lifetime of troubles. Carlin was working on the *Kraft Summer Music Hall* variety show for $1,250 a week as a writer and performer. He was auditioning for film and TV roles. It was the best time in his young life since going solo four years earlier in a career move that was inspired by the man from Mineola. They may have reminisced about their first meeting in 1960 in Dayton, Ohio (birthplace of Jonathan Winters). Brenda was working at the local racket club as a hostess. Since Carlin's star was rising and Lenny's was falling, it was as much a pilgrimage as it was a social call. It was the last time they saw him alive.

Mort Sahl also went to see Lenny in April of that year. The comedian was in a bad way. "He looked very, very sick," he told the *Los Angeles Times*. It was a tough reunion that left Sahl depressed. Sahl told Chuck Champlin, a writer at the *Times*, days after Bruce died, "We used to have a private thing. He used to say he was being crucified, and I went along with it. I'd say, 'Hey man, but don't forget the resurrection'" (*Los Angeles Times*, August 5, 1966).

Also in 1966, Richard Pryor and his girlfriend Maxine Silverman had packed up their stuff and driven from New York to Los Angeles. Pryor took a job as a recurring guest on the same show they hired Carlin to write for, *Kraft Summer Music Hall*, hosted by John Davidson, arguably one of the lamest performers on television. Pryor reckoned he could audition for roles in TV and movies by hanging out with the Tinseltown gentry at private clubs such as the Daisy. He was looking for an opportunity to cross over into movies and television, perhaps getting a series like NBC's *I Spy* that made Bill Cosby, his rival, a big star.

It's uncertain if Carlin or Pryor knew in advance that they would work together, but in the 2019 documentary *I Am Richard Pryor*, directed by Jesse James Miller, a clip from the *Kraft Summer Music Hall* features both comedians performing onstage with Davidson. They're all dressed in crewneck sweaters, white slacks and white shoes, the costume of the entire male cast on the show. Davidson, to look as hip as his clothes, asks both comedians to demonstrate the sound of their "favorite laughs." Carlin does the laugh of a staid individual, while Pryor does a perfect witch's laugh. It's an exceptional moment in the history of comedy to see two of the most important comedians onstage close to Lenny's Hollywood Hills retreat.

Richard Pryor's favorite routine by Lenny Bruce, according to biographer Scott Saul, had been "Airplane Glue" on his 1961 album

Lenny Bruce–American. Pryor loved the character in that story. Bruce assumes the part of a kid interested in sniffing glue but can't buy it without purchasing other things to cover for his habit. So in front of the shopkeeper, the kid says, "Gimme a nickel's worth of pencils, ju-ju beans, and two thousand tubes of airplane glue."

During America's restless postwar years, artists reflected the social, political, and cultural changes around them. They challenged the old, square order by producing work that was fun, free, and cool. In the United States, comedy was now moving "from the belly to the brain" in the words of educator Barry Sanders. The new generation of stand-up comedians dropped the joke telling for astute observations that made people laugh. They wanted to change minds, upset the censors, and peacefully revolutionize the world with *ideas* instead of weapons of mass destruction. Mort Sahl and Lenny Bruce were the presumptive leaders. Richard Pryor and George Carlin were among the disciples who spread the word.

Years later, Carlin learned that Bruce told many people that *he* would be his successor. Yet Lenny never told him. By 1966, Carlin was already pursuing a creative path of his own, inspired by Bruce. Recalling the first time he heard Lenny on vinyl in the PBS documentary *Make 'Em Laugh*, Carlin says, "[He] let me know that there was a place to go, to reach for, in terms of honesty in self-expression."

Jester (1962–1970)

Five

CARLIN'S CHARACTERS

When Carlin launched himself in 1962 as a stand-up comedian, it was according to his plan. The years he spent with Jack Burns, honing his stage skills and perfecting his ideas, had been a huge pay-off. Lenny Bruce and Mort Sahl were doing well, and Carlin believed he had enough material to join their ranks and compete for laughs. But he still had a long way to go to become as good as the comics he heard on the radio, such as Fred Allen. He had little in the way of repertoire, only some jokes left over from the Burns and Carlin show, a few impressions, and some great one-liners. He wanted to reach a wider mainstream audience, maybe even get a spot on television. Carlin learned that being a stand-up comedian would require patience, effort, and revision. So writing became his currency.

The first two years were full of creative highs and lows. One night, he would have the audience in stitches; on another, he'd be heckled. Carlin performed to drunken crowds or no crowds, as he did one night in Baltimore, Maryland, at a club called the Blue Dog. The club manager told him to go onstage just in case an audience showed up. The long list of gigs he kept in his diary was a like a day planner from showbiz hell. From the Colony Club in Omaha, Nebraska, to the Oakton Manor in Wisconsin, from the Copa in Cleveland, Ohio, to Springfield's Lake Club, Carlin realized how hard it was to be a stand-up comedian, onstage, alone with no props, no wigs, and no gimmicks.

Hitting the road and working as a solo act benefited from the help of Carlin's new bride, Brenda (Hosbrook) who was as quick witted and funny as her new husband. She and Carlin had married in June 1961. Born in Dayton, Ohio, Brenda had been working as a hostess at the local racket club where Burns and Carlin were performing. The two had immediately hit it off—a match of personalities, attitudes, and senses of humor. After a couple of long absences matched by lengthy phone conversations while Burns and Carlin toured America, George came back and proposed. Brenda gave him an unconditional "yes," and the couple got married in Dayton. Jack Burns, Mary Carlin, and manager Murray Becker were there as witnesses.

The pair went everywhere in the early days as Carlin finished up the club dates already booked for Burns and Carlin. When the duo split, Brenda traveled as her husband's biggest fan, attending shows where she was often the only member of the audience. Brenda and George moved to Chicago as a base of operations. There, Carlin would work the clubs within driving distance of the city while hanging out with his new, pot-smoking friends, the "folkies," who were supportive of his new, edgier material about many subjects, including politics.

Carlin worked for free at the open-mic sessions at Chicago's Rising Moon and the Earl of Old Town. Emerging singer-songwriters Steve Goodman and the late John Prine were two of the most eminent musicians to break out of the Earl of Old Town. Meanwhile, the Rising Moon club, which fell victim to an arsonist in 1963, provided the perfect setting for Carlin. He was among fellow, independent artists and college students who loved his brand of irreverent humor. He didn't depend on these gigs for the money; it was about taking creative chances to develop his craft.

Carlin drew in part on his experience as a deejay. He believed that if the characters could work on radio, perhaps they could work in front of an audience. It was a risk he was willing to take, having taken so many of them in the past couple of years. His characters would have contrasting voices, quirks, and plenty of New York attitude rooted in Carlin's personal life. He shaped the character of Willie West right out of KJOE. The fast-talking deejay who worked at W-I-N-O, "Wonderful WINO" he would sing, was right out of the Carlin handbook. Over time, the lineup got bigger with Al Sleet, the Hippy-Dippy Weatherman; Biff Burns, the sports reporter; and Bill Bulletin, the nasal-sounding newscaster. Carlin's female character, named Congolia Breckenridge came later. He was no longer alone onstage. He was fashioning himself as a modern-day jester in a nice suit by tapping into his personal life.

The word "jester" dates back to the fifteenth century, meaning "fool" or "one given to jests" as defined by *Merriam-Webster's* dictionary. The Fool in Shakespeare's *King Lear* comforts Lear with quips and banter; the challenge is to come up with the right words without insulting the king. If he could walk the fine line between mockery and satire, the fool had employment for life. And so it was for George Carlin.

One of Carlin's solo gigs was an appearance on the television show *CBS Talent Scouts* hosted by Jim Backus on July 17, 1962. Carlin shed the Jolly George mask and started fresh by talking about two types of humor: the old school, exemplified by Jack E. Leonard, and the new school, represented by Mort Sahl. Carlin mimicked the shtick of Leonard and the clever talk of Sahl. Closing with what he called "White House comedy," he stuffed his hands in the pockets of his sports jacket and did his stock impression of John F. Kennedy from his old act. In just six minutes, we see a confident twenty-five-year-old getting big laughs and generous applause for satirizing Vaudeville comics, praising hip comics (including himself), and making fun of the "present resident president."

At the end of 1962, Brenda became pregnant and moved back home to Dayton to have the baby with the support of her parents. Kelly Carlin was born in June 1963, making it a family of three albeit one dependent on a developing artist who wasn't making very much cash. It got so bad that they lived out of their car. Eventually, Carlin moved his new family back to the protected environs of Morningside Heights, borrowed money from friends, and got a tiny flat in the same building where he was raised, 519 West 121st Street. It was just a few floors away from his mother. Kelly talks about these tough years with great humor in her book *A Carlin Home Companion*. She says that her mother stayed by her father through it all. "I would never ask George to give up his dreams," Brenda wrote to a friend. "It's all he's got, and I really believe he can make it."

Carlin changed managers, replacing Murray Becker with Bob Golden, a musician from New York, to help get him work locally. (Becker's connections were stronger in Los Angeles.) Golden, whose own career was leading nowhere, took up the challenge because he had affiliations in the club scene. In the mid-1960s, New York was the hotbed of the folk era, chiefly in Greenwich Village, site of dozens

The Café Wha? In Greenwich Village, one of the most important venues for Carlin, Pryor, Klein, and Cosby. ROBERT K. CHIN—STOREFRONTS / ALAMY STOCK PHOTO

of music venues and coffeehouses where Carlin could do better than being on the road. He took part in open-mic sessions known as "hootenannys." Bob Dylan, Joan Baez, and Phil Ochs, to mention a few, staked their claim at these shows as the United States pursued a futile war in Vietnam. The younger, politically astute audiences were perfect for Carlin's routine that defied authority and made fun of the system. One of his bits was the commercialization of birth control pills, which, according to Carlin, could be advertised and sold like aspirin. The pills would therefore have catchy names like "Preg-Not" and "Nary-a-Carry." This bit didn't make any of his TV appearances until 1970 when he did the routine on Hugh Hefner's show *Playboy After Dark*.

New York's Bleecker Street was home to the Café Au Go Go, which opened in 1964, holding up to 230 patrons. Richard Pryor debuted there when the owner, Howard Solomon, booked him as a regular act. Carlin may have been on home turf, but his club competitor was turning heads and making people laugh. Pryor was on Bill Cosby's trail. He performed at the Café Au Go Go, the Improv, and the Bitter End before Carlin. (Cosby's big break came in 1962 at the Gaslight Cafe.) Pryor and Carlin had a collegial respect for one another, even sharing an agent for a while. Newspaper reporters and talent agents went to Greenwich Village to see the next big thing, and they were noticing Pryor. Cosby and Pryor had "hunks" or short routines they could perform on TV. Carlin needed to write one of his own hunks before he could land a booking.

Television in the mid-1960s was the backbone of the stand-up comedian. A good five-minute appearance on the *Tonight Show*, for example, could launch an entire career to millions of viewers. Another avenue was the new syndicated talk show circuit. This one featured daytime talk/variety shows that paid adequately with viewers in many TV markets in the United States and Canada. One of the biggest producers of the daytime talk show was the Westinghouse Company. It produced and distributed the *Merv Griffin Show*, the *Mike Douglas Show*, the *Steve Allen Show*, and the *Regis Philbin Show*—all worthy opportunities for Carlin to boost his résumé and be successful. Six months after Richard Pryor made his debut on the *Merv Griffin Show*, Carlin was booked, and he was ready. He had his initial character, the Indian Sergeant, and his first hunk. He came up with the routine during a round of writing at home and then developed the piece when he worked in the folk clubs of the Village.

Carlin's unique concept made the Indian Sergeant palatable despite its political incorrectness to some people today. The western movies he saw as a kid inspired the premise. Typically, in these B-movies, after the Indians raided a campsite or village, the townsfolk would receive a pep talk by a leading citizen or military man in order to fight back. That pep talk, in Carlin's scenario, might also apply to the Indians. The twist? Carlin's "sergeant" didn't come from Texas, he came from the Upper West Side of New York City. "This'll be the fourth straight night we've attacked the fort. However, tonight it will not be as easy as before: tonight there will be soldiers in the fort!"

Carlin performed the Indian Sergeant hunk for the first time on television in July 1965, the debut season of the *Merv Griffin Show*. Merv liked it so much on Carlin's first appearance that he asked him back to do it again on August 31. After the introduction from Merv, Carlin walks out and starts his routine: "I've been watching the westerns . . . an endless stream of them . . . and when the big scene comes . . . we never see how the Indians prepare for the ultimate battle." Carlin takes this story line and twists it into an original piece of thoughtful comedy, simple but effective, especially for a mainstream talk show for a mainstream White audience. What's notable is Carlin's sidebar in the introduction: "The Indians were good fighters. Just because they started in Massachusetts and wound up defending Malibu doesn't mean they were bad." Then he adds, "We really didn't play the game with them." He gets a nervous laugh with his provocative reminder of how indigenous people have been treated in America. Carlin made the commute from New York to Philadelphia to do the *Mike Douglas Show* with the same hunk.

In January 1966, Carlin got a job on the *Jimmy Dean Show* as a performer and writer. Bob Banner, the producer of the show, caught his act at Basin Street East in New York and was impressed by Carlin's Indian Sergeant routine. But it was on this program when Carlin tried an even finer demonstration of his expanding wordplay and delivery. It was a routine that came to him easily, culled from his radio days; he called it the "newscast."

The newscast bit had flexibility because he didn't have to memorize it like the Indian Sergeant routine. He simply read his clever wordplay and one-liners right off the page. As a bonus, he also incorporated commercial messages, and he invented two new characters: a sports reporter and a weatherman. On the *Coney Island Recordings* from 1948, issued in 1999, we hear Carlin as an eleven-year-old delivering a newscast. "Tonight we have news from Russia that Joseph Stalin has died during his sleep last night . . . looks like we're gonna win the war after all." By the time he appeared on television in 1966, Carlin had a fully realized character, rooted in his childhood.

Carlin appeared on the *Jimmy Dean Show* a month later. The jovial host clearly loved his new writer. Dean says, "I met him, for the first time, in the offices of the writers on our television show. He doesn't look like a comedian, but he is a funny, funny man." After Carlin takes a seat beside him, Dean continues in his charming, southern manner, "I'm tellin' you, you have furnished us some giggles 'round here. It's a pleasure to have you around." Dean sets him up nicely, saying that his audience often misses the evening news because they're at his show. Carlin pulls out a script from his sports jacket and launches confidently into the newscast: "And now the news with

Bill Bulletin. [higher, nasal pitched voice] Good evening, once again, the big hand is on the five, the little hand is on the six and it's time for the 11 o'clock report." Big laughs rain over him as he continues with the Biff Burns sports report in an even higher pitch: "Good evening fans, Biff Burns here in the Biff Burns sports light spotlight, spotlighting sports in the sports light, spotlight." Carlin is doing well. Then he throws it to Al Sleet, the Hippy-Dippy Weatherman, one of his most memorable characters, without missing a beat. "Hey baby . . . what's happening?" says Carlin, complete with sleepy facial expressions. He caps off the whole routine with Sleet's ridiculous forecast: "Radar is picking up a line of thundershowers from Utica, New York, to Middletown, however the radar is also picking up a squadron of Russian ICBMs, so, I wouldn't sweat the thundershowers . . . tomorrow's high, whenever I get up."

Al Sleet was Carlin's most personal character. He was a pothead weatherman fueled by cannabis, and Carlin was a pothead comedian. Sleet became an alter ego perfect for mainstream television. Audiences were curious about Al, a guy who was not one of them. He was a little strange but likable, and that was his most potent quality. Al Sleet probably reminded audiences of Bob Denver's portrayal of Maynard G. Krebs, the beatnik friend of the title character in *The Many Loves of Dobie Gillis*. Performing a "likable routine" on TV got Carlin steady employment. Agents loved him because they knew what to expect. He was charming, inventive, funny, and entertaining every time. Carlin even did a variation of his character on *Kraft Summer Music Hall* as Al Pouch, the Hippy-Dippy Mailman.

When Carlin performed on the *Tonight Show* on June 1, 1966, Johnny Carson shook with laughter during the Al Sleet routine. Carson just about fell out of his chair on the line "I wouldn't sweat the thundershowers." Carlin got the biggest laugh from the most influential man in show business. He would do more than 100 additional appearances with Carson, including Johnny's last season in May

1992. He even hosted the show in the early 1970s when Carson was on vacation. The newscast routine, capped with Al Sleet, was Carlin's stock-in-trade for many years, indeed, even after he altered his look. Here's a fragment from a 1972 *Tonight Show* appearance with Flip Wilson: "Good news from the Far East, no one was killed in Vietnam this week, however three people died of old age at the Paris peace talks." Carlin inserted topical material into his act with the newscast. He was funny without being preachy.

By the summer of 1967, Carlin's newscast routine was a feature on the CBS television variety show called *Away We Go*, broadcast on Saturday nights. It was a summer replacement for the *Jackie Gleason Show*, cohosted with singer Buddy Greco. Carlin got top billing as the cohost and head writer. Al Sleet made regular appearances, and Carlin wrote new material each week for the Hippy-Dippy Weatherman to deliver. In a clever move, in the August 5 broadcast Greco introduces Carlin with a newscast: "Two hundred years in the future." Al Sleet gives the weather for the solar system: "The high temperature of the day was 8,000 degrees, which was reached at the center of the sun. By the way, we'd like to give a big thanks and tip of the hat to the two guys who took that reading for us. We're going to miss them on our staff here."

Congolia Breckenridge was a female character that Carlin added to his routine called "Daytime Television." In 1967, he performed a seven-minute version on the *Ed Sullivan Show*, featuring voice characterizations of soap operas, game shows, commercials, cooking shows, and the always reliable newscast. The soap opera was called "Doctor Place." Life, love, and fooling around was the story. The game show, which featured Congolia, he named "Truth or Penalties," with the host, Guy Himself, a tougher version of the popular show *Truth or Consequences*. The setup is a reunion of Congolia with her sister, whom she hasn't seen in twenty-seven years. Congolia is a cross-eyed lady but dignified, a character who's self-aware. But she gets the answer to her question wrong, and they ship her sister back to Maine. It's a cruel result, but Carlin's act with all the TV ads, sound effects, and music bits easily rolls along.

Willie West was Carlin's exaggerated deejay, a character who showed off Carlin's remarkable ability to talk quickly without slurring his words. He re-creates the well-written phrases in *Last Words*: "1750 on your dial! Just above the police calls, kids! We got stacks and stacks of wax and wax, we're gonna pick and click the oldies-but-goldies, the newies-but-gooeys." Carlin was an excellent mimic of beeps, sirens, and electronic machines. The very sound of the broadcast comes right out of his mouth. The club version in the Roostertail in Detroit is on Carlin's first solo album, *Take-Offs and Put-Ons*. It's a delightful routine. Carlin sings original songs in a doo-wop style, with silly lyrics, and he includes original announcements with barely enough time to catch his breath. The character of Willie West highlights Carlin's deeper, one-to-one relationship with his listeners. His tone, timing, and humor made it sound like he was talking to one person at a time. That's how he built his audience.

On his second album, *FM & AM*, he kills with "Son of WINO" featuring Willie's replacement, Scott Lame, "the boss jock with the boss sounds from the boss list with the boss thirty that my boss told me to play. Right here on the nifty 850!" The routine follows up the Willie West character, beautifully repurposed five years after the original. This version, featuring all the sounds of a well-oiled AM radio, including its effervescing host, ended the characterization.

Six

George Lester Meets Cardinal Ignatius Glick

*C*arlin was the first to admit he was a lousy actor. He went to auditions for sitcoms, TV pilots, and motion pictures, a process he considered an ordeal. In an interview with Lawrence Linderman for the May 1973 issue of *Gallery* magazine, he says, "I went through nine or ten of those auditions . . . I remember the pain involved . . . that I was very, very self-conscious and knowing that I was bad, the biggest amateur in a group." According to longtime friend Bill Bennett, he took acting lessons with comic actor Charles Nelson Reilly that proved unsuccessful "because too much time was spent making each other laugh." If Carlin was to stick to his plan of becoming an actor, then he had to start somewhere, so he braved the nerve-racking audition process and landed two roles in the 1960s that launched his acting career.

Marlo Thomas was the daughter of Danny Thomas, one of show business's biggest stars. Her sitcom *That Girl* debuted on ABC television in 1966 and ran for five seasons. It was a hit, garnering Thomas four Emmy nominations as Best Actress in a Leading Role in a Comedy Series. The show's premise—small-town girl leaves home to make it on Broadway—had that dreamy appeal of lightness for audiences looking for escapist TV, especially during the Vietnam War. Thomas played a struggling actress, Ann Marie, an independent and energetic woman with unshakable determination. Each week, Ann Marie had to endure a different part-time job to pay the rent in between auditions. Her boyfriend was Donald Hollinger, a struggling writer, played by Ted Bessell. Over the course of the series, Donald and Ann's love for each other endures despite her unpredictable life in showbiz.

George Carlin auditioned for the character of George Lester, Ann Marie's agent in the fictional series. He debuted on November 10, 1966, in an episode called "Break a Leg," featuring Sally Kellerman and Dabney Coleman, future stars in movies and television. Carlin's role as the smart-ass agent may have been one of his least favorite experiences, but looking at his performance today, he's doing a lot better than he thinks. The role calls for George Lester to be an edgy, sarcastic guy, and that's how he plays it: "a bona fide agent" as Lester calls himself. Carlin's delivery is sharp, almost as if he wrote it himself. At one point, he looks at the camera with a self-conscious "get me out of here" glance. It's a pity the role wasn't recurring. Carlin brings his first-rate timing and cheekiness to the character without stealing focus from the other actors, especially Marlo Thomas.

His second supporting role came in Doris Day's last movie, *With Six You Get Egg Roll*, released in 1968. Howard Morris, whose claim to fame was the great 1950s variety program *Your Show Of Shows* with Sid Caesar, directed it. Carlin was much more agreeable about it, telling *Gallery* magazine, "I knew the part would be good, because although it was small, my character popped up in several places in the movie." He played Herbie Fleck in a comedy about a widow (Day) with three children marrying a widower (Brian Keith) with one daughter. The title of the movie stems from a line by one kid when the family goes to a Chinese restaurant. (As a large group, they get extra food with their meal.) Carlin plays a server at Ye Olde Drive Inn, meaning he had to be in scenes only when the couple met there privately. As with the character of George Lester, Carlin's delivery as Fleck was the perfect fit. He's a wisecracker, the sarcastic guy who can deliver a cutup. Carlin's five appearances in the screwball comedy add nothing to the story, such that it is, but he makes his mark in a movie that needs some verbal one-liners, especially during the chase scene in the last act.

So his two parts in the 1960s had him dipping his toe into acting and, according to his own assessment, suffering first-degree burns to his ego. Acting wasn't for Carlin because he knew nothing about it except through the motion pictures he watched as a kid. The movies of his youth created the impetus for him to try acting, but he never trained for it or understood a skilled actor's use of technique or movement. His work on *That Girl* and *With Six You Get Egg Roll* was a pleasant experience. He may have doubted his ability, but he never gave up on his dream of becoming an actor.

Ten years later, in 1976, Carlin appeared in the slapstick urban comedy *Car Wash* playing the part of a cabbie. Carlin wrote his own dialogue, doing the director and writer a big favor. It's a pity he doesn't share any scenes with Richard Pryor in the movie. In 1979, he narrated the universally panned satire *Americathon* directed by Neal Israel but otherwise shied away from the silver screen for quite some time. For the next few years, he continued to tour and to work in Las Vegas and on television until the time was right for him to take another stab at acting.

In an interview with *Playboy* magazine for the January 1982 issue, Carlin would reconsider his hopes to become a professional actor: "I think it would be really magnificent, about the age of fifty-five, to begin serious training as an actor." (He was forty-four at the time.) "I'd like to play small roles in out-of-the-way theaters, then get into films as an older character actor." Three years later, he enrolled in acting classes with Stephen Book. Book, a director, teacher, and author, had honed his coaching skills at the Juilliard School. He started his own workshops on acting in Hollywood in the mid-1980s.

Book met Carlin in 1985 when the comedian signed up for regular training. He wanted to work on his game. For two years, Carlin attended weekly classes, at first with his daughter Kelly, to prepare for movie and television offers that were coming his way. Stephen Book continued to be his coach for another fifteen years. "Being a great comic, he already had the natural instinct for creating funny characters and knowing how to give them their own voice," Book said. Why would someone so strong onstage suddenly feel uncomfortable working on a movie? The answer lies in the significant differences between the independence of working a stage solo and the collaborative effort of making a movie. As a comedian, Carlin was in control. Making a movie required him to give up that control, which for him was an enormous sacrifice, creating self-doubt.

Book identified four important differences for Carlin: "[There was] no immediate audience feedback in the moment, he didn't write what he is saying. Acting has to fulfill the intentions of someone else, the writer, and he was dependent on other actors and a director during his scenes." By understanding how moviemaking is a team effort, Carlin understood his role, as actor, in the process. Over time, Book could draw out the "actor" in Carlin by developing his improvisation skills: "George discovered that if he could improvise in character, he knew he had it and could bring him to life." He even road tested it. Once he had the character down, Book would invite him for walks in his neighborhood in Beachwood Canyon. Carlin would be in character and meet neighbors and strangers and start conversations. Book says, "Carlin was never recognized."

For Book, who calls his acting method "Improvisation Technique," Carlin was the perfect fit, giving the comedian just what he needed to excel as an actor. As Book describes it in his excellent tome *Book on Acting: Improvisation Technique*, published in 2002, it's "a technique of acting that is learned experientially" that relies on spontaneity, the most important element of improvisation. Book's method has its own rules, procedures, and applications that prepare an actor for any role, especially in television and film. Carlin endorsed the publication: "I was greatly in need of a teacher and a system which could bring out and begin to develop my natural skills in a short time." Carlin learned how to create a character, how to make choices based on the intentions of the writer, and how to be spontaneous while playing with those choices.

Under Book's tutelage, Carlin prepared for a big-budget comedy starring Bette Midler and Shelley Long that would be released in 1986. It was called *Outrageous Fortune* with Carlin in a supporting role as an ex-hippie, no less, named Frank, who lives on a reservation hustling tourists. On the surface, there was more Al Sleet in his performance, but the role and the production process didn't intimidate him. Book says, "When he arrived on the set he had a character that was created from the script as opposed to something he pulled out of his comedy backpack," adding that "every single scene had been rehearsed with me and we made sure we covered every choice." Carlin's dedication to the process paid off. As absurd as the movie's premise is, Carlin embraces the character of Frank, with excellent results.

Stephen Book says that Carlin's improvisation of the part astonished him when he appeared rarely for a session at Carlin's home in the Pacific Palisades: "George greeted me in the character of Frank, the tracker, to guide me into the house. By the time we got to the house, he sold me forty acres of the Pacific Palisades and a single horse . . . it was hysterical." Book was happy with his student's efforts. Carlin had learned Book's technique and was free to improvise in a character with intention, focus, and confidence.

Outrageous Fortune was a tremendous success for Long, who made a bold career move from television to motion pictures after quitting the highly successful *Cheers* on NBC. But what made it for Carlin was his association with like-minded creative artists. They and he shared a work ethic, comic sensibility, and a commitment to getting it right, making it an enormously gratifying experience. Stephen Book agreed. In his eulogy at Carlin's memorial in 2008, he

Shelley Long, Carlin, and Bette Midler. ©TOUCHSTONE PICTURES PHOTOGRAPHER: MICHAEL GINSBURG

recalled, "George was absolutely committed to learning a technique for acting and completely uninterested in being the class clown or star. He was in a new world and fearlessly accepted the challenge of not going for the laugh."

Carlin would reach a different kind of audience a few years later in the role of Rufus in *Bill & Ted's Excellent Adventure*, acting with Alex Winter and Keanu Reeves. Carlin played the straight man in this over-the-top comedy—a poor cousin to *Wayne's World* and *Ferris Bueller's Day Off*. The story is about two high school dimwits who have to come up with an oral presentation to pass their history class. They're rescued by Rufus, who has traveled from a future where Bill and Ted's music has ushered in a utopia. He loans the pair a telephone booth that can travel back in time so that they can kidnap famous people from history, such as Abraham Lincoln and Joan of Arc, to pass their class and become the saviors of the future.

The movie isn't trying to be anything other than its own, ridiculous self, which is endearing. Carlin's appearance keeps the story and the movie grounded because he's the only adult in the room.

When Carlin was asked to play the part of Rufus, he wasn't the producer's first choice. They were trying to get Eddie Van Halen, who is name-dropped by the lead characters, aspiring rock stars, in the film. Carlin says little about this role in his memoir, but he did discuss it with XM Radio host Sonny Fox in 2006, recalling that Reeves and Winter weren't exactly professional during the wait times on set. They continually joked around, and only when shooting a scene would they get serious and start working as actors. As Rufus reassures the audience at the end of the picture, "They do get better." He was right. He would return in 1991 to play the same role in *Bill & Ted's Bogus Journey.*

George Carlin plays the straight man in Bill & Ted's Excellent Adventure *with Alex Winter and Keanu Reeves.* ORION PICTURES CORPORATION/PHOTOFEST

That year, Carlin also starred in the little-remembered comedy *Working Tra$h* with Ben Stiller, who was just breaking out as an actor. The late Alan Metter, whose claim to fame was the financially successful lowbrow comedy *Back to School* starring Rodney Danger-field, directed the made-for-television movie. *Working Tra$h* was the first movie broadcast on the network's *FOX Night at the Movies* time slot on November 26, 1990. Andrew Sugerman produced it.

The movie is a "buddy picture" featuring two struggling jani-tors who work in an investment firm in New York. They get rich by acquiring inside information from the trashcan of a company execu-tive. (The shredder malfunctions so badly that no one can operate it.) Carlin is the lead actor playing the part of Ralph Sawatzky, a seasoned gambler who partners with Ben Stiller as Freddy Novak, a young, smart, and ambitious guy looking to become a broker. Leslie Hope plays the part of Susan Fahnstock, the established broker and love interest of Freddy. Veteran actor Buddy Ebsen plays the part of the senior executive of the firm, Vandevere Lodge. Another character, George Agrande, is Dan Castellenata, the voice of Homer Simpson.

The TV movie was a hit, garnering an eight-share audience rating in the United States. When it came out on DVD in 2004, Sugerman and Metter offered some revealing commentary on Carlin's process in preparation of the character, Ralph Sawatzky. First, Carlin chose all of his own costumes for the part, a mix of ill-fitting suits, shoes, and colorful outfits that look like they came from the closet of a dated Las Vegas casino host. Second, he polished some of his dia-logue with writer Tom Shadyac, a joke writer who directed several Jim Carrey pictures, including *Ace Ventura, Pet Detective* and *Bruce Almighty*. The results are remarkable. *Working Tra$h* is a tight, crisp, and heartwarming story despite the 1980s synth-music sound track.

Carlin's work is engaging, funny, and thoughtful. He based his accent on a New York sound he heard from local street cops in Morningside Heights. To fans of his stand-up routine, it was a familiar sound but with a little something extra. Carlin isn't doing a superficial impression. Sawatzky is a real, grounded character, and Carlin's efforts to bring him off the page reflect a true comic actor. In the DVD commentary, Sugerman says that Carlin "really dug the script" and "loved the character." He worked hard to learn his lines and prepare for the rigorous twenty-day production schedule while shooting *The Prince of Tides* at the same time. Apparently, production went long, and Carlin was often working one film in New York and getting a flight to Los Angeles to arrive on set the next day to work on *Working Tra$h*. That being the case, Carlin must have spent every waking hour learning his lines and preparing the character of Ralph Sawatzky literally on the fly.

The impact of Carlin's preparation and effort is evident on the screen. Frank is an honorable character who loves people and wants to spread his illegally gotten profits with friends, family, and the local orphanage. As Metter says, "George isn't concerned about comedy. He wants to play the character." Although Carlin says nothing about his participation and work on the picture, Sugerman ends the commentary with a personal note: "George called me [after the broadcast] to say how proud he was of his performance and that he was really pleased with it."

Carlin's first dramatic role was in the 1991 movie *The Prince of Tides*, directed by Barbra Streisand. She approached him to play the part of Eddie Detreville, a gay character who was a neighbor of Savanna Wingo, played by Melinda Dillon, twin sister of Tom Wingo, played by Nick Nolte. (Carlin traveled to Streisand's house to audition for her.) As Eddie, Carlin has four scenes running, about two and a half minutes of screen time, but he makes every one count. His first scene reveals everything we need to know about his character. Recently separated from a partner, he's feeling lonely. He was close to Savanna, who helped him through his breakup. In the backstory, Eddie discovered Savanna on the floor of her apartment attempting to kill herself. When Tom arrives from Georgia to his sister's New York apartment, he looks down at the bloodstained carpet. Eddie, looking glum, says, "It was a bitch washing it out." It's an exceptional moment. Carlin expresses the dark humor of the line without detracting from the seriousness of the moment.

Carlin's next three scenes in the picture offer nothing but comic relief. Streisand knew he could deliver a line to lighten the mood of her drama. In a doorway scene, the well-dressed Eddie discovers Tom trying to collect all the mail from his sister's mailbox, piling up after they put her in the hospital. Eddie looks over Tom's T-shirt and sweatpants and says, "This is not an attractive look for a middle-aged man," adding on exit, "Bloomingdale's on Saturday, big boy!" It's another charming moment in the movie for Carlin, whose natural delivery as a seasoned comedian never falters. By the time of his last scene, the audience, having endured the melodrama, needs a respite. Enter Eddie with baked goods into Savanna's apartment, where he discovers Tom and his psychiatrist, Susan Lowenstein (Streisand), enjoying a morning after, to which Eddie asks, "Did I interrupt something vile?," then asking Lowenstein, "Would you like a little butter on your croissant, darling?," clearly enjoying the double entendre of the question.

Carlin's work in *The Prince of Tides* is very good. The detailed coaching he got from Stephen Book prepared him to make the most of his four scenes. As the method-acting teacher, Stanislavski once remarked, "There are no small parts, only small actors." For this movie, Carlin's "small part" explored two important aspects of character development from a script: the basic core personality of the character and the basic attitude of the character. Book says that by discerning and taking on the core attitude of the character, "you create the character's personality." For the character Eddie Detreville, the attitude was "I'm lonely." In a follow-up conversation, Book was more specific: "[We] worked on transforming Carlin's body and personality, affecting his rhythm, pace, posture, inner life, and spontaneity so that he had a complete 'inside' and a complete 'outside.'"

William Grimes, writing in the *New York Times* in 1992, interviewed Carlin about the part: "He was written as an out-of-the closet gay [says Carlin] . . . I knew he wasn't a Marine drill sergeant trying to hide his gayness. The challenge was how to be a gay man acting effeminate but not be a cartoon or a stereotype." Carlin's focus on doing an authentic performance with depth came out of the workshops and individual coaching sessions with Stephen Book. It was a critically important gig. As he told Grimes, "Something happened in me. I had a sense of acceptance that I belonged, that I had something to offer. Whatever skills and talents I have finally gelled. I was able to get something out that I didn't have to push at, pull at, and yank at. I just felt, gee, this is going right."

Four years later, Carlin was cast in what he considered the role of a lifetime in the TV miniseries *Streets of Laredo* from the novel by the late Larry McMurtry. The series premiered on November 12, starring James Garner, Sissy Spacek, and Sam Shepard. Carlin played the part of Billy Williams, donning a period costume from the American West. He was fifty-eight years old at the time and is a natural to play the part: independent, defiant of authority, and irascible. Stephen Book said that Carlin "prepared his fifteen scenes by finding and creating the character and then focusing on the individual scenes and how his character served the emotional purpose of each scene. In this way, Carlin was prepared with emotional choices and transitions for every moment of his scenes." Billy Williams is an empathetic character in the movie set in 1895. He drinks a lot, walks with a limp, and is in love with Maria Garza, played by Sonia Braga. She is the mother of the chief protagonist, Joey, her unstable son, who's on a killing spree along the Texas–Mexico border.

Carlin's performance is emotionally broad and sincere. When he expresses his love for Maria, his quietness pulls you in. It's an important story point in the picture that while Maria, a widow with three children, is attracted to Billy, their relationship runs deep yet unrequited. When Maria dies, Billy loses it painfully, expressing his profound loss while acting out. At her burial, Billy sings with Lorena Parker (Spacek) over the grave. It's a lovely scene.

Three years after the release of the miniseries *Streets of Laredo*, writer-director Kevin Smith approached Carlin to play a part in the 1999 movie *Dogma*, a satire of organized religion, in particular Catholicism. Smith was a big fan of Carlin's works and his vocal skepticism of religion. The offer came after the death of his wife Brenda; falling into a state of depression, his daughter Kelly says in her autobiography *A Carlin Home Companion*, "I knew he was struggling emotionally. He looked tired and didn't seem to have the vigor he usually had about his work." Smith, whose claim to fame was the low-budget, independent comedy *Clerks*, wrote a part specifically for Carlin to play, Cardinal Ignatius Glick. The big-budget comedy features a self-centered leader of the Catholic Church in Red Bank, New Jersey (Smith's hometown). Who better to play the part of a man who's in the news for his "Catholicism Now" campaign?

In the first few minutes of the film, Carlin appears as Glick at a press conference outside the steps of St. Mark's Cathedral. Glick's plan is to rebrand the church with a new image of Christ. Instead of the "wholly depressing image of our Lord crucified," says Glick, he says we need a "booster." Glick introduces us to the "Buddy Christ," featuring a small statue of Jesus Christ standing with a huge grin, with an extended right hand pointing out and its left hand showing thumbs-up with a wink in its eye. Glick says it "pops" and is far more appealing than a crucifix.

Smith's opening shot at Catholicism featuring Carlin in full costume is his way of letting the viewer know this movie is going all out to make fun of organized religion and religious belief. It makes sense to see the man in the role who admitted on *Class Clown*, "I used to be a Catholic. Now I'm an American." Who better than the antiestablishment comedian to play the high-ranking cardinal in a movie about Catholic doctrine? For Smith, who considered Carlin's output a worthy substitute for his own religious ambiguity, he was the perfect choice.

Carlin appears three times in the movie. Like his work in *Prince of Tides*, he makes a powerful impression. His second appearance in the third act features a brilliant speech by Glick defending the doctrine of the Catholic Church, and Carlin knows he's in on the joke by punching up his lines with vigor. His preparation with Stephen Book was re-created in Book's manual about acting, citing the opening speech with Carlin's notes. Beside each section of his opening monologue in *Dogma*, we see the actor's choices: earnest, distasteful, assured, reverential, and so on, marking out Carlin's "choreography" of the speech, as Book puts it. Carlin's dedication to acting resulted from his commitment to preparation. Once he learned a system for acting technique, he was confident in front of the camera. All of his self-doubt vanished. Stephen Book's coaching served Carlin very well over the course of his acting career. It would lead to some decent work in Smith's *Jersey Girl* (2004) as Ben Affleck's father, an edgy, working-class parent who was tough on his son.

Smith was impressed by Carlin's dedication to acting. In 2010 at the tribute to Carlin, produced by the New York Public Library, he said, "He fucking loved acting, that's the thing probably a lot of people didn't know about George. You see him in his element, you watch him in the clips, and he's a brilliant master at it, but my God, he loved acting so much. That's what he wanted to do most in life was be an actor, and he'd say that on set."

For Smith's next movie, *Jersey Girl*, Carlin gets a part specifically written for him, but he was unimpressed. The character, in his mind, had little backstory. So he prepared one for the character Bart Trinke, father of Ollie, played by Ben Affleck. Smith remembers,

"Kevin, I just want you to know, there's a character named Greenie, that I'm always fighting with. . . . He goes, 'all right, the thing is what's not there on the page is you never say why I'm always fighting with Greenie, but like what I want you to know is I've come up with a backstory for myself about why I fight with Greenie all the time, and I wrote it down, I committed it to memory, and I've since thrown it out, it will never come up in your movie, but I want you to know that if you need me to reference something, I'm going to pull it and that's where the words are going to come from.'" Smith was so impressed by Carlin's work that he always asked him back for bit parts. Unfortunately, Carlin's tight work schedule often conflicted with Smith's movie schedules.

George Carlin is not remembered today primarily as an actor. Yet ever since he was a little boy, starry eyed and enchanted by silver screen heroes such as Danny Kaye, it had been a dream. Roles in critically derided movies such as the horror-farce *Scary Movie 3* and *Jay and Silent Bob Strike Back* may not have won him any awards, but he brought undeniable talent and energy to every role he played.

SEVEN

CARLIN'S ACT OF CREATION

*A*nthony Lane, theater reviewer for *The New Yorker*, once wrote, "Experiences of value can be safely stored, accruing interest, and awaiting retrieval in maturity" (March 1, 2021). Lane was commenting on a recently published biography of English playwright Tom Stoppard, whose extensive body of work, in Lane's observation, matured as he did. It was the same for George Carlin. We can examine the evolution of his creativity through his albums, his TV appearances, his movies, and his books. He had no finish line as an artist.

So how did he do it? How did George Carlin bring it all together? He had a plan that morphed into a practice. His life, career, and work were in steady revision. The farther he positioned himself from the world, the more prescient he became. He turned his observations into words. The more he wrote, the funnier he got, and the funnier he got, the more philosophical he became. His late years were rich, filled with wisdom accrued after years of bucking the system. He enjoyed life, and he loved to learn, especially from his friends.

Two of those friends were Bob Altman and Paul Krassner.

Altman was from North Newark, New Jersey, and he met Carlin around 1964. Born in 1931, Altman grew up in a mostly Italian neighborhood, where, he said, "they used to play, 'Catch the Jew.'" Altman took music at school and worked part-time as trumpet player. He went to Syracuse University to study economics but didn't finish his degree. He was more interested in the performing arts, so he enrolled in the prestigious Manhattan Neighborhood Playhouse. He studied acting with Sanford Meisner and dance with Martha Graham. Altman thrived under their tutelage. In 1955, he graduated from the University of Miami with a degree in drama, but the acting jobs were few and far between. Following in his father's footsteps, Altman enrolled in the Wall Street School of Finance to take a few courses in moneymaking. He excelled at the school, leading to a job with McDonnell & Co., a brokerage firm in Newark.

Altman put his skill set to good use as a financial analyst. He was able to decipher the cryptic language of money-speak for his clients. In those days, he was known as a "customer's man." He spoke to investors in plain language, told them where their money was going and how they would profit. He thrived for seven years before taking another shot at acting in 1962. This time, he took a leave of absence from his lucrative job for a year and was cast in plays from Illinois to California. The work was good. He played Oswald in *King Lear* in Miami and Bill Starbuck in a Newark production of *The Rainmaker*. (Burt Lancaster got wide acclaim for his portrayal of Starbuck in the film version of 1956.) When he returned to full-time work, he took acting classes at night and kept his day job.

Altman met George Carlin when he hung out in the coffeehouses of Greenwich Village, the hub of folk singers and poets. Carlin was married with a young daughter in tow, living a hand-to-mouth existence in those days. Altman and Carlin enjoyed each other's company, occasionally smoking pot. The pair often met at Moylan's Tavern on Broadway, shooting pool, drinking beer, and sharing war stories about their struggling careers. Then one day in 1968, Carlin was doing an opening set at the Café Au Go-Go, and the headliner canceled. When the manager asked Carlin to do a second set, he refused but recommended his friend Bob Altman instead. With his friend's endorsement, Altman accepted on the spot. Years later, he remembered his debut to Canadian reporter Kevin Prokosh: "I did twenty-five minutes. I kept making observations and people laughed" (*Winnipeg Free Press*, May 23, 1986).

Altman assumed an irascible character named "Uncle Dirty" and started working in Greenwich Village as a stand-up comedian. Only one album exists by Uncle Dirty. It was released in 1971 on the folk label Elektra. It was recorded in performance at the Gaslight in New York, mainstay for Bob Dylan, George Carlin, and Bill Cosby in the 1960s. Uncle Dirty was an edgy guy who talked about identity politics and the American education system. On the album, Uncle Dirty weighs in on a variety of topics, including dating, mescaline use, and nuclear war. Altman's style is a lot like Carlin's. He's smart with his words, but he's not as polished. "The American eagle has two wings," explains Uncle Dirty, "a left wing *and* a right wing. If they don't flap together, the bird falls on its ass."

Altman introduced Carlin to an important book he was reading at the time: *The Act of Creation* by Arthur Koestler. It was published in 1964. Koestler was born in Budapest, Hungary, in 1905. In 1914, his family moved to Vienna, Austria. There, he attended university, studied engineering, and held a variety of jobs in Paris and London. He got a job as a correspondent for the British newspaper *The News Chronicle*. While on assignment, he was captured during the Spanish Civil War and charged with espionage by the Nationalists led by General Franco. He was given a death sentence. His wife, Dorothy Ascher, lobbied the British government to have him freed. Months later, he was released.

Koestler's time in prison left an indelible mark on his life. He left the news business and turned to writing. His first novel, *Darkness at Noon*, released in 1940, was based on his years in Spain. Originally published in German, the English version was a huge success in its day, the closest rival of which was *1984* by George Orwell.

Koestler also wrote books about psychology and human behavior. He was especially interested in how the brain worked in creative

Arthur Koestler, author of The Act of Creation. PHOTOFEST

people. The result was *The Act of Creation* (1964), a study of the process of human invention in the arts and sciences. Like physicist Albert Einstein, Koestler was going for a general theory of human creativity. From "The Logic of Laughter" to "Some Features of Genius," Koestler lays out a complex theory that Bob Altman absorbed. He was so enthused about Koestler's engaging ideas that he had to share them with his friend, George Carlin.

Koestler said the art of creation is "fluid, without borders or divisions," and that "the jester should be brother to the sage." His book explains how comedy needs associative context to be successful and that laughter is a "reflex" to relieve the tension of that context. He called it a "matrix" illustrated by an image of an empty chessboard. Altman's recommendation stuck in the curious mind of his friend.

Carlin adopted some of Koestler's ideas. On the *Charlie Rose* program, broadcast March 26, 1996, on PBS, he talks about it: "If the jester says something funny, he's a jester. If he says it in marvellous language, then he's a bit of a poet. If there's an underlying idea underneath the well-put, funny line . . . he becomes a philosopher." *The Act of Creation* was not just another book that helped Carlin understand the deeper, philosophical meaning of his craft. It was his mission statement.

*

As the culturally charged 1960s unfolded, George Carlin's political humor developed at the same time. As a high school dropout, to paraphrase Paul Krassner, he never let his education be spoiled by higher learning. By the time he was thirty, Carlin realized he wasn't as politically informed as the under-thirty crowd, aka the counterculture, whom he wanted to entertain. On one level, he likened himself to attitude and irreverence, but he didn't have the political gravitas to integrate as an artist.

A voracious reader, one of Carlin's most important influences on his political thinking was *The Realist*, an original publication of satire and "free-thought criticism" edited by Paul Krassner. It debuted in July 1958 for thirty-five cents, featuring Krassner, a journalist with a self-described "pathological resistance to authority." In his memoir *Confessions of a Raving, Unconfined Nut* (2012), Krassner tells his fascinating story with a great deal of charm and wit. Satiric writing was something rare in American culture in the 1960s as he tells it. While Mort Sahl and Lenny Bruce were onstage talking about the absurdity of American politics, Krassner was writing about it. *The Realist* became the print equivalent of a stand-up routine yet broader in subject, a niche publication without ads and dependent on subscriptions and newsstand sales. One of its subscribers was George Carlin.

Paul Krassner was born in Brooklyn, New York, in 1932. He played violin from an early age, making his Carnegie Hall debut in 1939 at age six. It was an auspicious moment for the young boy, who got a laugh when he used his right leg to scratch an itch on his left—*as he played*. His mother, Ida, was born in Russia and moved with her family to New York when she was an infant. His father, Michael, was born in New York of Hungarian ancestry. He was a printer by day, a short-order cook by night, and a music lover entering his middle son into violin lessons at age three. Krassner's older brother George also took lessons, and the pair often practiced at home and under the tutelage of Mischa Goodman. The brothers also performed for hospital patients and Jewish community events. But it wasn't all that rosy. As Krassner recalls in his autobiography, "I must've practiced myself out of childhood."

Krassner spent his school days "skimming" from class to class doing the bare minimum to pass and advance from one grade to the next. He says he read nothing to "hinder his independent progress" as a student. Nevertheless, he finished high school, then took journalism at Baruch College in New York. It was his way to avoid military service and to write for the college paper, *The Independent*, whose editorial policy at the time was anticensorship, which perfectly aligned with his political sensibility. He also started performing as a stand-up comedian with the stage name Paul Maul. His act was a mix of satiric commentary, joke telling, and violin playing, reaping financial and artistic benefits (as small as they were).

While in college, Krassner met Lyle Stuart, a dynamic journalist he considered his "media guru." In 1951, Stuart published a monthly magazine called *Exposé*, later renamed *The Independent* in 1956, best known for its muckraking humor and adult-oriented stories. He hired Krassner to write ads and draw cartoons for the paper. One of Krassner's cover stories for the periodical was about the requirement of draftees to sign off on a list of 600 subversive organizations the military believed were unsuitable for its personnel. This "Loyalty Program," as it was known, infuriated Krassner because he believed it violated a person's right to assembly. Stuart agreed and published the article in *The Independent* as its lead story.

Stuart was a big fan of *Mad* magazine on its debut in 1952 and immediately started a subscription by writing to the publisher, William (Bill) Gaines. By sheer coincidence, Gaines was a charter subscriber to *The Independent*, so when the two met, it led to a lifelong friendship and business association. Stuart moved his office to the seventh floor of the *Mad* building on New York's Lafayette Street, and there, Krassner befriended Gaines and started writing for *Mad* magazine.

When Krassner started *The Realist* in 1958, he got vigorous support from Steve Allen, Groucho Marx, and Lenny Bruce, who became one of his closest friends. Bruce supported the publication with gift subscriptions, inviting Krassner to give away copies at his Town Hall concert in 1960 to get the paper into the hands of his fans. This was the first time Krassner met him. A few years later, when Bruce wrote his autobiography for *Playboy* magazine,

Paul Krassner, circa 2007. His satiric publication The Realist *was a creative inspiration for Carlin's social commentary.* MEDIA PUNCH / ALAMY STOCK PHOTO

Krassner was hired as editor. Krassner's love of comedy matched his passion for self-expression, and Lenny Bruce encompassed the best of both worlds. Bruce was getting into taboo subjects such as abortion rights, the legalization of marijuana, and nuclear testing at the same time Krassner was writing about them.

Krassner was at the Gate of Horn club in Chicago in 1962 when Bruce was arrested for using profanity onstage. George Carlin was at the same performance and arrested for not having ID. According to Krassner, Bruce had fifteen arrests on obscenity charges from 1962 to 1964. It was to him an absurd and unjust series of arrests that eventually ruined Bruce's health and career.

In his book, Krassner describes the cultural change of the mid-1960s as a "mass awakening" after World War II: "encompassing sex, drugs, and Rock 'N Roll, was at its core a spiritual revolution . . . where psychotropic drugs became a sacrament, sensuality developed into exquisite forms of personal art, and the way you lived your life showed the heartbeat of your politics." *The Realist* pursued these ideas with gusto, pushing Krassner, as a reporter, into the middle of the culture. He hung out with the charismatic leader of the movement, Abbie Hoffman, and LSD enthusiasts Timothy Leary and Ken Kesey. He later moved to San Francisco, the center of the entire counterculture movement. By 1968, he was the de facto satirist, giving the unforgettable nickname for the Youth International Party, "Yippies," led by Jerry Rubin. But all along, Krassner's priority was getting *The Realist* published every month. He practically worked for nothing, especially during the early years, ensuring he paid his contributors first. He supported himself with freelance work and stand-up comedy.

In 1969, Carlin met Krassner during a recording of *The Smothers Brothers Comedy Hour*. Krassner's publication and his fearless writing style that took inventive shots at the hypocrisy of the government, religious institutions, and the law impressed him. The kids may have had *Mad* magazine, but the young, college-educated adults had *The Realist*, a paper whose sole aim was to defy authority, question mainstream news stories through satire, and offer alternative ideas about politics and culture. It was dark, funny, and irreverent. (*The Realist* ceased publication in 2001.)

Krassner saw the world through the lens of absurdity, and his intelligent satiric writing appealed to Carlin. He said he liked *The Realist* because it "made important arguments in relentlessly funny ways." Krassner's writing inspired him because it helped him focus his own ideas about the world, refreshing his act. Carlin's choice to self-educate opened him up to a wide variety of publications from which he could learn. If Lenny Bruce proved it possible to take a position as a rebel comedian, Paul Krassner showed, in print, an intelligent, provocative way to look at the world. As a result, Carlin found a better way to express himself onstage and in his books. Paul Krassner died in 2019 at eighty-seven.

*

In the silence and darkness between the stars, where our Sun appears as just a particularly bright star, a theorized group of icy objects collectively called the Oort cloud coast along their orbits like lazy moths around a porch light. —NASA

George Carlin was no lazy moth. By changing his orbit and leaving the system, he sought creative freedom. The outcome, if there was one, restricted his craft. So he chose the Oort cloud as his imaginary office circling around the planet. As he said to Charlie Rose, "I've decided that if you really stay in it [the system] and think there's a solution, you're part of the problem" (November 23, 1992).

When he was filming *Working Tra$h* in 1990, Carlin carried in his back pocket a map of the solar system. During breaks in the shooting, he would pull out the map, show it to his fellow actors and crew members, and talk about it. Andrew Sugerman, who produced the movie, was impressed by Carlin's enthusiasm for the cosmos. To Sugerman, Carlin's gift as a comedian was his ability to "filter all of his self-education into his politically incorrect comedy [and] make it work through the filter of blue-collar stand-up" (commentary track to *Working Tra$h* [2004]).

Carlin's journey to the Oort cloud started when he was a kid, although he didn't know it. But he did know that he could make kids laugh without being caught by the teacher when he went to work. For the ten-year-old Carlin, who was encouraged by his mother to make people laugh when he was four, it was easy. He vowed to become a comedian at the age of fifteen because he felt the healing power of laughter wash away his loneliness.

By the time he reached high school, he was regularly entertaining his friends and family. In his twenties, when he was a deejay introducing rock-and-roll music to young listeners, Carlin invented characters to channel his ideas. Performing as Al Sleet was fine for a while, but it wore him out. Sleet was a one-dimensional character played by a multidimensional artist. But Carlin was only in his thirties when he discovered this. He felt the change but didn't have the wisdom. Dropping acid in 1969 was the game changer. As time went on, he kept asking questions, gaining knowledge and insights about the world around him.

When Carlin turned sixty-six, in a conversation with author David Jay Brown in 2003, he admits his art bloomed as he did: "Over the years I noticed that what occurs as you age is an accumulation of information, data, knowledge, and what I'm going to call the matrix of the mind" (*Conversations on the Edge of the Apocalypse* [2005]). The aging process was a means to an end for Carlin, a way of producing better, more refined ideas in his writing. He gained hindsight and spatial distance. Like a dedicated basketball player, Carlin was a gym rat constantly working on his game, perfecting his punch lines. He wrote constantly, creating files on his computer in the dozens and assembling endless combinations of words and phrases that spoke to him. He combined wit, humor, rationale, and logic, often in the same sentence.

By choosing to self-exile from the human race, Carlin was free to create without roadblocks. When he did, as he writes in *Last Words*, he did so with the aim of reflecting back to humanity exactly "how fucked up they are." He goes further with author David Jay Brown. Carlin says, "His task [the jester] was to trick the gods, to humor the gods into laughing, so that there was access to the divine, because laughter is a moment when we are completely ourselves." But he didn't reach that conclusion overnight. It took a long time. "No one is more himself than the moment when he's laughing at a joke . . . that's when you slip in a good idea," he said to David Jay Brown.

"I like them to know *I'm thinking*. Then I like to show them that."

The beauty of reading and listening to Carlin today is to hear an artist fully engaged in his profession. We remember him because of his commitment to creativity and being open to revision, where the *real* writing is done. In his last interview, he said to Jay Dixit, "When I sit down to consciously write, that's when I bring the craftsmanship. That's when I pull everything together and say, how I can best express that? And then as you write, you find more, 'cause the mind is looking for further connections" (*Psychology Today*, June 2008).

Carlin was always on the job. In *Psychology Today* (June 2008), he said, "I have a network of knowledge and data and observations and feelings and values and evaluations I have in me that do things automatically." Working in this thoughtful way brought him a lot of satisfaction his entire life: "You get so much pleasure finding good observations and finding which things are the richest things you can say, that probably the brain remembers how that happened and learns to provide the best stuff." Carlin's books and HBO shows reflect the sweet maturity of his craft.

Consider this random sample of Carlin's late works, called "That's the Spirit" from *When Will Jesus Bring the Pork Chops?* (2004):

> I don't understand these people who call themselves spiritual advisors. Franklin Graham, the unfortunate son of Billy Graham, is George Bush's spiritual advisor. Bill Clinton had Jesse Jackson.
>
> Here's the part I don't understand: How can someone else advise you on your spirit? Isn't spirit an intensely personal, internal thing? Doesn't it, by its very nature, elude definition, much less analysis? What kind of advice could some drone who has devoted his life to the self-deception of religion possibly give you about your spirit? It sounds like a hustle to me.

This excerpt features the philosopher at work: an opening statement that he's thinking about "spiritual advisors," citing two examples, then a broader question regarding one's faith followed by new questions that are openings for laughter, closing with the punch line that the U.S. presidents, Clinton followed by Bush, are being "hustled."

Everything is up for debate in those two paragraphs: faith, leadership, doubt, self-discovery, and their relationship to religion and politics. Is this the trickster calling the shaman black? Not on the surface. It's a keen, self-educated observer who's weighing the possibilities of suspicious behavior in people who, in this case, have "spiritual advisors." The beauty of this piece is its timelessness. Substitute any recent American president—Obama, Trump, or Biden—and you'll get the same hilarious result.

In his 1984 HBO special *Carlin on Campus*, he merges the "Lord's Prayer" and the "Pledge of Allegiance" in a perfect juxtaposition of church and state. Carlin believed that the clergy manipulated people to keep them in line, while the traders convinced people into thinking they had freedom of choice. Religion and capitalism are two of Carlin's most consistent topics in his work. Another of his works brings these coherent ideas together. He called it his "Patriotic Suite," and it can be found on his last HBO special, *It's Bad for Ya.*

The piece is actually a series, "Proud to Be an American," "God Bless America," "Takin' Off Yer Hat," "Swearing on the Bible," and "You Have No Rights." On this "suite," Carlin connects the dots of American jingoism, the national anthem, flag-waving and the so-called constitutional rights of every citizen. From Carlin's distant perspective, he finds absurdity in one of America's most prized values, patriotism.

Carlin opens with a question: "I saw a slogan on a guy's car, and it said *proud to be an American*. And I thought: what the fuck does that mean? I've never understood national pride. I've never understood ethnic pride . . . pride should be reserved for something you achieve or attain on your own. Not something that happens by accident at birth." At first glance, that conclusion seems ordinary, but for Carlin, it comes from his deeper examination of the use of language, political expediency, and the systemic brainwashing required to make it all stick. His sharp observation isn't superficial. It has philosophical weight. He sees the absurdity of rituals in the American system and deconstructs their meaning like Socrates in the middle of Athens: "Does it matter which hand is on the Bible when I'm swore in? What would happen if I raised my left hand? What if the Bible was upside down? What if the Bible was missing pages?" The farther he goes, the more the audience begins to question the value of belief in the first place. He takes us by the hand, keeps us laughing every twenty seconds or so, allowing us to reach the same conclusion.

Carlin's greatest work, a masterstroke of wordplay, is *A Modern Man*, which opens his third book and his thirteenth HBO special, *Life Is Worth Losing*. It's three and a half minutes of pure Carlin: an onslaught of twenty-first-century jargon, buzzwords, clichés, and slogans all delivered in a perfectly written monologue. To hear it is uplifting. To read it on paper is profound:

> I'm a modern man
> Digital and smoke-free;
> A man for the millennium.
> A diversified, multi-cultural,
> Post-modern deconstructionist.
> Politically, anatomically and ecologically incorrect.

And that's just his opening volley! In the rest of the piece, Carlin amasses his best list of English-language expressions collected during his lifetime. It's so good, so in the pocket linguistically, and he did it because he saw the world from the outer edges of the galaxy. The steady arc of his life and work can be summed up by his great advice, written in the preface to *When Will Jesus Bring the Pork Chops?*: "Just keep movin' straight ahead. Every now and then you find yourself in a different place."

It worked for Carlin. Maybe it could work for us.

Eight

WELCOME TO HIS JOB

Despite his successes in the 1960s, George Carlin was growing weary of characters like Al Sleet and deejay Willie Wise. Sure, they were fun to perform and paid well when he did them, but he was feeling unsatisfied. Carlin was experiencing an artistic conflict, he told Lawrence Linderman in 1973: "My mimicry and the ability to write jokes for these characters carried me to a big success on television that had nothing to do with the kind of rapping, me-to-you things I was doing at the coffeehouses" (*Gallery*, May 1973). He continued, "I decided I wanted to be the best writer-comedian I could be, and so the first thing I had to do was change what I was doing." That change in his approach would brim with his love of words, some of which you could not say on television. He hoped the audience would come along for what he knew might be a bumpy ride.

In 1968, Carlin was signed to a three-year contract at the Frontier Hotel in Las Vegas, owned by the eccentric millionaire Howard Hughes. The contract paid him $10,000 a week with a raise if he was successful, and he was. Carlin would typically work three-week engagements every few months. He opened for mainstream singers such as Robert Goulet or Al Martino, headliners who entertained tourists by the busload in those days. One night, Carlin was asked to do a private show for golfers in the Howard Hughes Invitational. It's not known if any members of the PGA were in attendance, but there were plenty of amateurs, and when they arrived, they were already drunk and obnoxious. Carlin did his regular show at this event, including a new, personal talking point: the size of his ass. "If you look at me sideways, I go from the shoulder blades right to the feet. Straight line. No ass." It was a tough crowd, but he finished his set, the first of his two-year contract. Afterward, the operations manager Robert Maheu approached him and said that the bit and his multiple use of the word "ass" offended some people in the audience. So he took Carlin off the show, paid him for the week, but, in an unusual move, did not cancel his contract. By doing so, Maheu inadvertently set the stage for Carlin's notable return.

It's January 25, 1969. Carlin makes his second appearance on the *Jackie Gleason Show* from Miami. The first thing you notice is his look: he's wearing a tailored, double-breasted blue suit, but his hair is longer, and he's sporting sideburns. His seven-minute routine is his take on television. He says that regularly scheduled morning TV shows never get Emmy Award recognition. He cites *The Farm Report* and *Sunrise Semester* and the national anthem, which TV stations played when they signed on. But he's setting up a more subversive bit. Carlin takes the premise further with his late-night invention, "The J. Edgar Moover Show, with Ramsey Clark and the FBI orchestra, the Joe Valachi Singers and some of the most sought-after people on television." In the clever routine, Carlin takes a shot at the Justice Department and the FBI's leader, J. Edgar Hoover, by mocking Hoover's corny sense of humor: "I just came from a stakeout; that's a backyard barbeque . . . ha, ha ha." He finishes the routine with Moover's reminder: "Join us again tomorrow night when our guest might be someone hiding out near you. If he is, tune us in; turn him in; and drop out of sight." Carlin had twisted the famous Timothy Leary phrase "tune in, turn on, and drop out" to finish his monologue. Leary, a psychologist and LSD proponent, might have been amused. But the FBI wasn't.

On January 22, 2009, an Associated Press story reported that the FBI, in fact, had started a file on Carlin in 1969. (Carlin was one of many artists and performers to have their own FBI file.) The file had twelve pages, including a memo that stated, "His treatment was in very poor taste and it was obvious that he was using the prestige of the bureau and Mr. Hoover to enhance his performance." But Carlin's indirect reference to Leary was revealing. If he was to change his act by unleashing the best writer-comedian within, drugs were going to become part of the mix.

In October, Carlin dropped acid for the first time, which he would later describe as an experience that changed him. It affected his mood and quieted his anxiety, especially before a show. He was in Chicago when he was booked to play Mister Kelly's, one of the city's most vibrant jazz clubs. In his memoir *Last Words*, Carlin fails to mention from whom he got it, but he does report that he took it many times over the course of his two-week engagement. He called it an epiphany: an awakening of his inner poet. He noticed the slight changes in his outlook and what other possibilities regarding his art he could explore. Equipped with this valuable insight, he pressed on to Washington, D.C., and then to New York for a gig that expressed his acid trip.

In December 1969, Carlin was booked at the ritzy Copacabana club in New York for two weeks. Jules Podell, rumored to be connected to Frank Costello, crime boss for the Luciano family, managed the club. Podell hired Carlin on the condition that he would do a clean act and not the unruly one he recently performed at the Frontier Hotel. That guarantee came from Carlin's booking agent, Irvin Arthur. Carlin took the gig but saw it as an opportunity to liberate himself from his jester persona. During his engagement in front of a straitlaced audience, Carlin performed what he later called a Dada-style set. It was his way of poetically flipping the bird in the face of the showbiz establishment while transitioning into the thoughtful poet he wanted to be. He dared Podell to fire him while onstage and, in a move that would make Lenny Bruce proud, lay underneath the piano, describing what he saw. Podell was not impressed, and Carlin got his wish. After three agonizing weeks, the Copa finally released him from his contract.

In his excellent book *Comedy at the Edge* (2008), author Richard Zoglin asked Carlin about his experience at the Copa: "Toward the end of my act, they slowly turned my light off. . . . And they took the sound down at the same time . . . very dramatic . . . it was almost sweet in a way. And I knew I was free." Carlin was turning away from the royalty he had served in the past. His physical appearance was about to change, too. In a symbolic move, he would shed his jester's costume—black suit, white shirt, and skinny tie—and headed back to Los Angeles.

In the spring of 1970, when Carlin was admitted to the hospital for a double hernia operation, Kelly Carlin, Brenda and George's observant eight-year-old daughter, witnessed her dad's transition from the clean-cut stand-up comedian to the bearded, ponytailed artist we know today. "He went in my Daddy, a clean-cut man with groovy sideburns and came home someone else: a man with a beard. A beard he would not shave for the rest of his life" (*A Carlin Home Companion*).

What happened in that hospital? His mobility limited, it's safe to assume that Carlin reconsidered his place in the world. With no pot to smoke or acid to drop, he concluded that performing as a jester rang false. Now off the scene, it was the perfect opportunity for Carlin to take a chance and reinvent himself. He was thirty-three years old and "on the wrong side of the generation gap" as Richard Zoglin put it. But he was still in the service of the Vegas king, Howard Hughes.

In September, Carlin returned to the Frontier, opening for the Supremes. He was feeling good, but once again, one night he had to perform in front of a mostly male audience, which consisted of salespeople for Chrysler, the carmaker. By 1970, Vegas was booming as a hub for conventions by big business. This wasn't a crowd from the liberal East ready to accept and enjoy provocative entertainment. It was more like the Copa crowd. After months of working fresh material into his latest performances, Carlin was bracing to spring a new piece on Vegas. It was short and effective: "Down the street, Buddy Hackett says shit. Redd Foxx says shit. I don't say shit. I *smoke a little of it*, but I don't say it" (*Last Words*). This subtle observation got Carlin fired. The Frontier canceled his contract at a huge financial loss for Carlin of $12,500 a week. Frontier management said he "belabored the audience with four-letter words." That brief routine may have revealed Carlin the poet, but it didn't win him any lucrative contracts in Vegas.

In November 1970, Carlin hit the road. At a performance in Lake Geneva, Wisconsin, they booked him to perform at the Playboy Hotel. A new singer fresh from the Broadway production of *Fiddler on the Roof*, Bette Midler was Carlin's opening act. What she and the audience witnessed would go down in showbiz history as a public display of Carlin's metamorphosis. At the show, he got some massive pushback from the audience when he started talking negatively about the Vietnam War. One man, who was a veteran, stood up and challenged him with a fist raised in the air. The spectacle was too much. Carlin lost the crowd, chastised them, and marched offstage through the club and out the front door. Carlin returned to his hotel room to settle himself. While there, a mere hour after the messy show, he got a telegram. The manager of the club said he breached his contract, so it would not pay him. In a veiled threat, the manager suggested that for his own safety, he should leave the hotel immediately. Midler told author Richard Zoglin, "I just remember being so shocked that they would let him go, because I thought what he was doing [onstage] was perfectly reasonable" (*Comedy at the Edge*).

Carlin was out $1,300 for his weekend engagement. With no Vegas money coming in, coupled with his nonpaying gigs in coffeehouses, he couldn't afford the loss. So he drove to Chicago to see Hugh Hefner and ask for his money. Hefner, who once backed him and Jack Burns for their irreverent humor, said no. Carlin was aghast. He couldn't believe that the guy who supposedly stood for freedom of expression, the man who regularly booked Lenny Bruce, was that cheap. Word spread about the Lake Geneva debacle in the show business trade magazine *Variety*. Carlin's manager, Bob Golden, and his agent, Craig Kellem, couldn't handle the adverse publicity or their client's frustration, and they agreed to a split. Carlin then hired Jeff Wald and Ron De Blasio to manage his bookings. Wald saw a new Carlin emerging, later telling Richard Zoglin, "I saw something underneath. He looked like a guy trying to escape" (*Comedy at the Edge*).

Carlin worked night after night in small clubs and coffeehouses, honing his craft without the safety net of his familiar characters. He also took a pay cut. Wald worked hard to book him into the Greenwich Village clubs that once supported up-and-coming comics like his client, but they still considered Carlin a Vegas act. Having seen his old act, they thought he was too straitlaced for the scene. He persevered. With a new management team in place and the encouragement of his wife Brenda, Carlin was soon donning blue jeans, sandals and tie-dyed shirts onstage, leaving his earlier persona behind.

For the next couple of years, Carlin hit the reliable talk show circuit, performing new (clean) material and telling the world that he was no longer in his old act. He had garnered favor from Merv Griffin and Mike Douglas over the years, and they were happy to support Carlin's self-made reinvention. After all, he was still one of the funniest comedians in show business. As he cycled through the programs, in a cathartic move, he opened up about the changes in his look and work. If the TV hosts could accept him, maybe the mainstream audience, which was probably surprised by his physical transition, could too.

In May 1971, Carlin finally got the approval he needed during a performance at Santa Monica College. They booked him at the last minute to replace Mort Sahl. The college crowd loved his new routine and rose to their feet after his performance. "This is what I aspired to," he told Richard Zoglin, "such affirmation of what I believed about myself." Carlin felt accepted and relieved. His choice to let go of the suit and skinny ties paid off. Two months later, he recorded his transitional comedy album at the Cellar Door in Washington, D.C., *FM & AM*.

Carlin's breakthrough onstage came with a light, personal poem called "The Hair Piece." He presented the work during most of his appearances in 1970. "I'm aware some stare at my hair. In fact, to be fair. Some really despair of my hair." It's an accessible, charming recitation featuring a simple rhyming scheme: hair, fair, care, debonair, mon frere. By 1971, Carlin regularly performed "The Hair Piece," including it in a spot on the *Ed Sullivan Show* in February. It was his eleventh and last appearance on the show, which CBS later canceled in March. Carlin was now gaining confidence in his material, fusing the tried and true of his pre-acid days with new ideas. "The Hair Piece" was personal, and he blended the poem into his regular act. It was also his way of letting the audience know he was embracing his new look. Besides the poem, his last *Sullivan* routine included commentary on the Vietnam War and Muhammad Ali, who was making a big comeback against Joe Frazier after being kicked out of boxing for refusing to go to Vietnam: "So the government said, if you won't kill 'em, we won't let you beat 'em up." He closed with a weather forecast from Al Sleet, the only character he continued to perform.

Sullivan staffers censored Carlin's performance following the dress rehearsal on the morning of the broadcast. In an interview with Dick Cavett in 1992, Carlin said he was going to include a joke about Alabama Governor George Wallace and his phrase "pointy-headed intellectuals," a pejorative on the elite class he regularly used. Carlin posed the question, "Have you ever seen the shape of those sheets on the heads of those people down there?," clearly linking Wallace with the Ku Klux Klan. When the producers heard this during the rehearsal, they gave Carlin a choice to do either the "Ali" joke or the "Wallace" joke but not both. He chose the former, but he thought it was a strange way of censoring his act (*Dick Cavett*, 1992). "The Hair Piece" was less likely to upset the older fans while appealing to younger ones.

Most of his TV appearances between 1967 and 1972 reveal Carlin the jester becoming Carlin the poet. Many of the talk show allies who recognized Carlin's artistic move agreed. Mike Douglas recalled seeing Carlin at the *Rooster Tail* club in Detroit. In his memoir *I'll Be Right Back* (2000), Douglas says Carlin's first set "drew only a mediocre response," and after a break, he "returned to the stage with a vengeance." It was at this show that Douglas probably heard the "Seven Words" piece for the first time, showing, for him, a critical change in the comedian's routine. Writes Douglas, "It was shocking, but shockingly funny as well."

Carlin appeared many times on the *Mike Douglas Show* before *and* after he changed his look. In 1972, when *FM & AM* was released, Douglas recalled the Detroit gig during Carlin's appearance on the program. Of the change, Carlin says that "it made him more efficient as a person rather than spending time worrying about things that were not important," adding "that I'm in control in terms of what happens to my life and career" (*Mike Douglas Show*, February 18, 1972). John Lennon, who was cohosting the show, chuckled when Carlin admitted he "wasn't in his own act." The ex-Beatle, whose band broke up a mere two years earlier, could relate.

For an artist, the "crux of the biscuit," to quote Frank Zappa, is the process of working on expressing deeper ideas in a piece through revision. For George Carlin, the material consisted of words. Like good sourdough, he kneaded the phrases, clichés, and euphemisms and arranged them into his act. "His ideas needed to be contained," daughter Kelly notes in her memoir. "Everywhere in our house . . . there were pads and pens in every room so that when an idea popped into his head, it had a place to go" (*A Carlin Home Companion*). Carlin developed his own filing system and categorized subjects into themes. He would assemble and then disassemble in a process of constant revision. He was distinguishing himself not as the comedian who *writes* his own material but as the writer *performing* his own material. "I think of myself as a writer," he told *Psychology Today* in 2008. "First of all, I'm an entertainer; I'm in the vulgar arts. I travel around talking and saying things and entertaining, but it's in service of my art and it's informed by that."

After several challenging years, Carlin reinvented himself. He did it by pushing the boundaries of his craft, and, like the universe, he expanded. The 1960s jester shed his black-and-white costume and stopped serving the king. He blossomed as a colorful, introspective poet for the 1970s. Introspection and the fertile soil of the English language would provide ample supply. He never knew this as the class clown, but as he matured and continued to educate himself, he found his identity. Perhaps he heard the voice of Thalia, the muse of comedy, when he told Linderman, "I see things that strike me as funny, and I pull them out of life and put them into words" (*Gallery*, May 1973).

Poet (1971–1989)

Nine

CARLIN ON VINYL

*A*t the 1970 Grammy Awards, the trophy for Best Comedy Album went to Flip Wilson. He won for *The Devil Made Me Buy This Dress* on a label called Little David, founded by Wilson and Monte Kay in 1969. George Carlin was probably amused. He had met Wilson in the summer of 1966 on *Kraft Summer Music Hall* with Richard Pryor. All three worked on the show as writers, enjoying the sun, making people laugh, and, once in a while, snorting cocaine.

Flip Wilson's specialty was his seminal female character Geraldine Jones, the outgoing and independent southern woman who's line "what you see is what you get" endeared him to millions of fans. Monte Kay promoted jazz musicians in the late 1940s, including Miles Davis, Charlie Parker, and Erroll Garner. He knew talent when he saw it. Kay met Wilson in California in 1966, becoming his agent and later his business partner with Little David records. The story from the Old Testament featuring the underdog David slaying Goliath, the giant, in a single fight inspired the label name. The Little David logo depicts the triumphant hero with his slingshot.

Wilson's biggest break came after years of working the Chitlin' Circuit in front of Black audiences. Like so many comedians who came before, including Carlin, Wilson's appearance on the *Tonight Show* in 1965 brought him notoriety. Redd Foxx endorsed him and Wilson soon made a prime-time appearance on the *Ed Sullivan Show*. He took full advantage. He and Kay approached NBC to produce a one-hour comedy special in 1969. The program was a hit, so NBC hired Wilson and Kay to produce a weekly prime-time variety show the following year. Wilson was no fool. He knew his show needed an edge. Comedy on television was changing, led by the works of Norman Lear, whose sitcom about a bigoted character named Archie Bunker would expand the boundaries of topical humor. *All In The Family* debuted on January 12, 1971.

So Wilson hired Pryor and Carlin as writers. Carlin also performed on the variety show, which lasted four seasons until slumping in the ratings at the end of 1974. Wilson's slump wasn't unique. Variety television, such as the *Carol Burnett Show*, was losing audience share to more edgy sitcoms, such as the aforementioned *All in the Family* and the *Mary Tyler Moore Show*.

Carlin was performing in the coffeehouse and nightclub circuit with his new look and act. His manager Jeff Wald knew Monte Kay from his New York days. They often smoked weed and shared showbiz horror stories. With the Grammy win, Wilson and Kay had enough incentive to offer George Carlin a record deal, albeit a modest one. Wilson talked about it during his appearance on the February 29, 1972, episode of the *Tonight Show*. Signing Carlin to Little David records, Wilson said, was "an opportunity for George to feel freer as an artist and for me to be a part of, maybe, helping a guy that I admire."

And help him, he did.

Carlin had a few advantages. He was working his new act in clubs, making steady TV talk show appearances besides gaining new fans by appearing on the *Flip Wilson Show*. Carlin's contemporary look appealed to a younger, suburban crowd. The *Wilson* show debuted on September 17, 1970, on NBC. Wilson was among the few Black artists to host his own show, but with a solid writing team, a big budget, and a lineup of guest stars each week, the show pulled in big

Carlin's transitional album.

ratings. They nominated it for eighteen Emmy Awards, winning two, in its first season.

A year later, riding the wave of his popularity on television, Carlin would begin a fruitful, six-album career on Little David. Wilson and Kay's gamble was about to pay off big time.

Recorded over two nights at the Cellar Door in June 1971, *FM & AM* was George Carlin's coming-out album. Like two contrasting radio frequencies, the title is symbolic: loud, commercial AM versus cool, alternative FM. When the booking at the Washington, D.C., club was confirmed, Carlin wrote new material, polished his words, and "killed it" in the comfort of a small venue and a gracious audience. In a full-page ad for the record in *Billboard* magazine, Carlin is quoted as saying, "I felt true acceptance by an audience."

FM & AM is perfectly balanced: five tracks on each side and a simple, agreeable jacket design. Nothing fancy here, just a couple of images of Carlin, relaxed, sitting on a metal stool in front of a blue canvas backdrop. Two variations of the image would make up the cover of *Class Clown* released nine months later. For the audio file, the AM side is in mono, while the FM side is in stereo.

Carlin gets right to the point with his story of being fired from a casino, the Frontier, for saying "shit" onstage in a place where the patrons can play "craps." The album's opening salvo captures the comedian on a roll: "Shoot is shit with two Os," he exclaims. Deconstructing the English language will thread all of his forthcoming work. He recites "The Hair Piece," first heard on the *Ed Sullivan Show* in 1970, followed by his keen observations about "Sex in Commercials" using his twisted voices and what he calls "filthy slogans" heard in them.

"Drugs" has us thinking about the abundance, use, and health effects of common drugs such as aspirin and caffeine. He talks about diet pills as well as birth control pills in a bit he wrote in 1967, including catchy brand names such as "Preg-Not," "EmbryNo," "Nary-a-Carry," "Mom Bomb," and "Junior Miss." He closes the set doing a two-character phone call about a couple that gets pregnant, inspired by the great comedy team Nichols and May, who had their routine called "Mother and Son."

Side 2, or the AM side, has five routines that Carlin mastered when he was "in his old act." The fast-paced "Son of WINO" reflects his radio days, and "Divorce Game" satirizes the game shows, like the *Newlywed Game*. He resurrects Raoul and Congolia Breckenridge, a pair of characters who have to determine the custody of their children. His hilarious self-taught Ed Sullivan impression follows this bit. It's easy for anyone to do, Carlin says, by keeping it simple:

introduce the most bizarre acts you can think of, and you'll be great at house parties. Carlin was one of the last stand-up comics on *Sullivan*, which had recently been canceled.

He closes the album with "The 11 O'clock News," a tried-and-true hunk that never failed to get laughs. Carlin's cleverness with sharply written headlines and high-energy characters was his stock-in-trade in the mid-1960s. We even hear from Al Sleet, the Hippy-Dippy weatherman, "tonight's forecast: dark!" After years of struggling to get out of his old act, *FM & AM* marked his successful transformation. The album reveals a thoughtful, confident, and funny man happy with his new act.

Ironically, Carlin thought he had bungled the performance. It should have been the culmination of all his hard work and preparation, and a clear expression of his perspective on the world, but he felt he'd ruined his big chance. The pressure he felt to break out in a fashion that suited him was hard to define at first. Fortunately, the appeal of the album nullified any doubt regarding his creative change in look and direction. The album went to number thirteen on the Billboard 200 album list. It sold more than 500,000 copies, reaching gold record status and garnering Carlin's first Grammy Award for Best Comedy Album. The committee nominated it with Cheech & Chong's *Big Bambu* and labelmate Flip Wilson's *Geraldine*. Carlin had nothing to worry about.

If there's one record that most comedians point to that made them choose stand-up as a career, it was his next album, *Class Clown*. It stirred one young comic to learn it word for word and another to jump on board and pursue the so-called vulgar art as a vocation. Comics, critics, and historians would point to it as a revelation, citing Mark Twain as Carlin's closest rival in satiric commentary. For George Carlin, it would launch the third phase of his career like a Saturn V rocket to the moon.

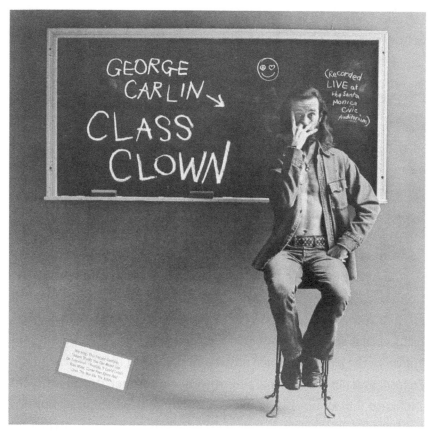

Carlin's most influential album.

It was recorded at the Santa Monica Civic Auditorium on May 27, 1972, a couple of weeks after Carlin's thirty-fifth birthday, and released in September. As a clue to the contents, the jacket design features the comic with a finger up his nose and a warning regarding one of the more potent tracks that "could infect your mind, curve your spine and lose the war for the Allies." It's a bold statement for a bold album. He's in a larger venue, too. At 3,000, it was one of the biggest concert audiences in his career, but Carlin has no trouble reaching the back row. His life as a deejay, addressing one listener at a time, is about to pay dividends.

The entire album is a trip back into the comedian's early life. Carlin reveals everything he did as a kid in grade school on the album's title track, "Class Clown." For him, it was an easy gig: the artificial fart under the arm (among many other versions), nose humming, playing with your head or throat with your fingers tapping your voice box, and cracking your knuckles and popping your cheek. Part of the record's appeal is Carlin's shared experience as the class clown. He gets big laughs re-creating what it was like to be with him in school, only this time in a classroom in Santa Monica. His commitment to "Bi-Labial Fricative" (sounds produced by both lips by a puff of air) is irresistible.

The seminal track is the last one on side 2, "Seven Words You Can Never Say on Television" a routine that would stick to Carlin for the rest of his life. The recording marked the first time he presented the piece onstage after crafting the introduction, selecting the words, and commenting on their use. It's a work based on a list, one of Carlin's favorite templates. In the 1982 *Playboy* interview, Carlin says that the premise of the piece came from his own childhood. "When I was a kid, nobody would tell me which words not to say. I had to go home and say them and get hit."

Carlin spent years gathering a list of so-called dirty words as early as 1950 when he took up the habit of noting his favorite phrases. He discusses it extensively in *Last Words*. One of the first was "longhair fucking music prick," which he heard his friend say while beating up a Juilliard music student in the street in Morningside Heights. The second was slightly meaner, "Kraut cunt," spoken by another friend regarding a Mrs. Kohler, a neighbor. By the time he joined the air force, he heard a fellow serviceman say "burly, loudmouthed cocksucker" and added the lyrical phrase to his list. The "seven words" hunk came from Carlin's diligent effort to organize his thoughts into set pieces. A third of his act was built with an exploration of the English language. Euphemisms, clichés, slogans, and misnomers were among his favorites.

Patton Oswalt, writer and comedian, called the seven words "a machine-gun burst": shit, piss, fuck, cunt, cocksucker, motherfucker, and tits. Carlin says it so fast on the album it sounds like one word. Then he slowly takes the longer phrase and breaks it down into its components. To some people, the best part is the setup: "There are four hundred thousand words in the English language and there are seven of them you can't say on television. What a ratio that is! Three hundred ninety-nine thousand nine hundred and ninety-three to seven!" Carlin's logic, and it's a sound one, frees the seven words of their offensive meaning. Fifty years later, these words grace TV comedy and drama shows freely.

Comedian Colin Quinn, a fellow New Yorker, called *Class Clown* "the Sgt. Pepper of Irish Catholics, releasing psychological pain." He paid tribute to Carlin in 2020 on the National Comedy Center special *Laughing Matters: Carlin's Legacy.* Quinn's reference to the Beatles' influential recording shows the impact Carlin's album had on his life. He considered Carlin "a holy man" in style and substance. Quinn was engaged by Carlin's take on Catholicism in bits like "Special Dispensation," in which he critiques the entrenched rites of the Catholic Church beautifully using the language of the religion against itself.

On side 2, Carlin takes a step back and sees the world as an outsider. He had learned in Corpus Christi school that asking questions was one of the best methods of gaining knowledge. He loved those early years and fondly remembers the men and women who taught him the importance of independent thinking. Yet it doesn't stop him from mocking God. "How can he be perfect? He's not. It shows in his work . . . everything he ever makes dies." Richard Zoglin points this out in *Comedy at the Edge* (2008): "His vivid account of his Catholic school days was a masterpiece of autobiographical vaudeville and theological criticism."

The album had the same impact on actor-comedian Denis Leary, who heard it when he was in high school. He was an altar boy in

Worcester, Massachusetts, at St. Peter's Catholic Church when he found out that *Class Clown* was listed in the church bulletin as being off-limits to parishioners. So he and his fellow altar boys pooled their money and bought a copy. Leary told the story at PBS's 2008 *Mark Twain Prize for American Humor* show honoring Carlin: "We went to this kid's house whose parents were away, specifically, to the 'Seven words' track, and it was at that moment that I became an ex-Catholic, ladies and gentlemen." He adds, "That was when I realized you could make money for saying stuff that my dad used to say when the car didn't start." In 1993, Leary released his debut comedy album, *No Cure for Cancer*, a hyped-up series of topics right out of the Carlin playbook: drugs, smoking, and America's infatuation with guns.

Jay Leno went a step further in his appreciation of the record: he *memorized* the first track. In his autobiography *Leading with My*

Jay Leno, circa 1975. PHOTOFEST

Chin (1996), Leno says, "I would run it through my head before making extemporaneous class speeches at Emerson [College], just to jump-start myself. I'd have his comedic rhythm playing in the back of my head: a proven, wonderful rhythm that I tried to emulate."

Leno was twenty-one when the record came out. He was floating around college doing shtick with his roommate, Gene Braunstein, in Boston's coffeehouses. When he broke out on his own, starting in strip clubs, he would open with the "Class Clown" routine and segue into his own stuff. Leno says that his biggest influence was Robert Klein, yet the boldness of covering Carlin says a lot about the power of *Class Clown* and Leno's bravery doing a routine he didn't write or experience. Carlin's record pushed him to do his own routines based on his own life experiences during his years at Emerson College.

Tom Papa, comedian and actor, felt something deeper. He says that he understood the notion that being a comedian was a job. As he told Jenelle Riley in 2004, "That was the first time that I ever got the concept, [that] there are some grown-ups that do this" (*Back Stage West*, February 26). Papa, who got his big break opening for Jerry Seinfeld in 1995, has an illustration of Carlin on the wall of his office to remind him of the importance of working at his craft. As the author of several books, five stand-up television specials, and a radio show on SiriusXM, Papa's work ethic has paid off, just like his idol.

The sales for *Class Clown* were brisk. The album went gold and peaked at number twenty-two on the Billboard 200, spending more than seventeen weeks on the chart.

The Circle Star Theater in San Carlos, California, was the site of Carlin's third Little David album, *Occupation: Foole*, recorded over two performances from March 2 to 3, 1973. The stage was circle in the round, with the 3,700 seats no farther than fifty feet away. They powered the stage to rotate during a performance, although Carlin had it locked, allowing him to move instead. The physical aspect of Carlin's act was critical to his presentation. A move, usually comprising a facial expression, augmented his presentation. This round stage worked for him, like the one he performed on in Phoenix for his second HBO special in 1978. Unlike *FM & AM*, this record sounds like a continuous performance, reflecting Carlin's train of thought. His ideas easily segue from one topic to the next.

Carlin ingratiates himself with his audience immediately: "Welcome to my job . . . nobody goes right to work . . . screw the company, the first twenty minutes belong to you, right?" This was Carlin's go-to opening for a few years. Later, he would use what he called the sledgehammer effect: an earth-shattering opening line usually formed as a rhetorical question.

Carlin's cocaine album.

Occupation: Foole was Carlin's "cocaine" record. The design with multiple images of him in a series of crazy positions only enhances the pumped-up mood he was in. Success was measured not only in dollars but also in lines of cocaine, which Carlin admitted made up the bulk of his recreation in between shows. The jacket to *Foole* with its oversize head shots and multi-images of Carlin in a yellow tie-dyed shirt looking wild all point to that crazy time in his life.

The performance, thankfully, is much more grounded. The routines on here are further explorations of his ideas from *Class Clown*. This time, he includes a nuance: making another kid laugh to draw attention away from the source of the laughter. That kid would be kicked out of the classroom or asked to explain to the teacher what's so funny. Carlin relishes the power: "If you were really good, you could clear the room." Actions have consequences, and if you could say something funny, you got a laugh. If you could do it with purpose, training, and style, you had an occupation, hence the title.

For the first time, Carlin talks about his neighborhood, which he called "White Harlem," and his doo-wop groups in the hallway, leading to a bit called "Black Consciousness." As a guy who soaked in the culture of his 'hood, Carlin was comfortable talking about the use of the words "negro," "colored," and "Afro-American" by comparing those words with "whitey," "haystack," and the mysterious "Caucasian," the last, Carlin says, sounding "like a shoe style" or a mountain range. The track "New York Voices" is rooted in Carlin's keen ear for accents, dialects, and street talk. "Childhood Clichés" is a piece about a parent's warning, such as "you'll break your neck!" His experiences are not exclusive; they're shared. Everything he developed as a deejay—energy, diction, and pace—comes to fruition on this performance recording. His ability to speak to a large audience yet make it feel one to one was getting better.

Carlin's "Filthy Words" extends his list of dirty words you can't say on television to include "fart, turd, and twat." But he has given more thought to exploring all the different uses and euphemisms for "shit" and the word "fuck" that hang people up the most. He says, "Fuck leads the double life. It means love and life *and* is used to 'hurt' each other." The whole routine informs and entertains.

Occupation: Foole was nominated for a Grammy in 1974, went gold, and solidified Carlin's place in the comedy world. It also drew the attention, indirectly, of the Federal Communications Commission (FCC) when it was played on WBAI on October 30, 1974, just after the release of the album. (More on this in chapter 10.)

The release of *Occupation: Foole* marked a trio of albums whose sales put Carlin on the cultural map. It took six weeks to peak on the Billboard 200 chart at number thirty-five, not bad for a spoken-word album up against the top music albums of the year. In less than two years, from February 1972 to the end of 1973, Carlin had three hit records, an impressive run by any measure. Kay and Wilson were amused, but the success of Carlin's first three records didn't match his next three.

Recorded in the Paramount Theater in Oakland, California, *Toledo Window Box* was the first in which Carlin goes all out on recreational drug use, especially marijuana. It was released in November 1974, the same year as Cheech & Chong's *Wedding Album*, Richard Pryor's *That Nigger's Crazy*, and Robert Klein's *Mind Over Matter*, all nominated for a Grammy Award. Carlin's album missed the cut, yet they certified it gold.

The title track, "Toledo Window Box," is about his experience as a drug user. He follows up with "Nursery Rhymes," alluding to Snow White and the Seven Dwarfs and the drugs each one of them was on: "Happy was into grass and grass alone," "Sleepy was into reds," "Grumpy? Too much speed," "Sneezy was a full-grown coke freak,"

"Doc was a connection," "Dopey was into anything," and "Bashful was paranoid on his own."

The track "Some Werds" is Carlin's collection of weird, paradoxical phrases, such as "military intelligence," "semi-boneless ham," "guest-host," and "jumbo shrimp." He always had something to say about the way humans communicate, but on *Toledo*, the words fall off: "Sometimes I just say shit I've never heard before." He's not crossing any lines on this record except for the track "God," which looks at Catholicism. Carlin is settling for less on this record. His piece "Snot the Original Rubber Cement" is well thought out but silly when heard today, like most of the cuts on this album, that pales compared to the truly impactful "Seven Words" routine. He closes with "A Few More Farts", material here reincorporated on the 1978 HBO special because "fart" was added to his list of filthy words. Given these conditions, this record has no focus beyond the memorable title, a reference to a strain of marijuana.

At the end of the debut of *SNL*, which Carlin hosted, the comic makes a point of holding up the cover of his latest album, *An Evening with Wally Londo, Featuring Bill Slaszo*, by way of promotion. The album, his fifth for Little David, was recorded at the University of Las Vegas on March 18, 1975, and released in October of that year, days before his *SNL* appearance. The cover design features a huge close-up of Carlin's face staring at a ticket graphic in the top left corner. The back cover is a tiered image of about three dozen "Carlins" in blue. His second monologue on *SNL* is on the album. "Y'Ever" is another rhetorical question-and-answer routine, including "What do dogs do on their day off?"

Instead of a casino recording, Carlin and producers Monte Kay and Jack Lewis chose a college where Carlin had the most impact as a performer. Even with the unusual title, it was in Carlin's wheelhouse. He opens with "New News," re-creating his newscast bit without the character, Bill Bulletin, to deliver it. (He uses the piece in his first

HBO special two years later.) Carlin admitted that this record had "no concept at all," yet his material is strong and his delivery superb on "High on the Plane," his take about smoking dope on a jet. We hear echoes of Lenny Bruce in the pace of his delivery, rhythm, and speed. "Bodily Functions" is another example of Carlin's microworld analysis, resembling *Occupation: Foole*: "We don't take a shit or take a piss, we *leave* them!" His best piece is "Baseball-Football," a comparative study of the two sports using common expressions that distinguish them: "In football we have sudden death. In baseball we have extra innings; we don't know when the game is going to end."

Then he makes a poignant remark about religion, saying, "Religion is like a lift in your shoe. It's important sometimes and helps you walk straight for a while, however long you need it. That's the secret . . . just don't make me wear your shoes if I don't want 'em."

Despite the clever title that rolls easily off the tongue, Carlin's fifth album for Little David didn't reach the same sales figures as his previous efforts. That said, *Billboard* magazine named him Comedy Artist of the Year in the spring of 1975.

During the late 1970s, Carlin's drug use caught up to him. He couldn't deliver at the top of his game like he used to, hooked on a drug that affected his voice and messed up his life. His coke habit went on for so long that he referred to it as his "cocaine years." He went on long binges, often lasting for days. He talked about it with Sonny Fox in 2006. Recalling his *SNL* debut after a six-day bender, "You can hear me grinding my teeth." Nevertheless, the cocaine years had its benefits: self-discovery and revelations about his life and his relationship with the larger world. But it didn't kill him. As he told Judy Gold in an interview at the 92nd Street Y in 2001, "My abuse and overuse of drugs was considerable. But it always had a built-in line to it . . . you could sense the danger in it, and that was part of the attraction, but there was a self-limiting thing about it." Carlin didn't arrive at this inner world without some inner discovery of his own. The poet was aiming for something deeper to explore.

His subjects changed. Carlin wrote and performed material that was now about introspection. He called it the "microworld" or the "little world" of human activity. It was the world we all shared. Despite the subjects he explores, such as vegetables, snot, and assorted bodily functions, Carlin gave himself permission to discuss the naval-gazing topics that were important to him, and he didn't have to look very far to find them.

On the Road, Carlin's sixth and last album for Little David, arrived in April 1977, two years after *An Evening with Wally Londo*. The jacket features an image of Carlin adding a smile to a chalked body outline on a highway. Considering his slide in sales and his ongoing cocaine habit, you could say he was imagining the death of his career. The back cover of the album features a humorous plea to the potential buyer: "I'm glad you came over here to the comedy section before you took off" [from the hot pop section]. He talks about an eight-page libretto inside and that "George does fourteen minutes on 'Death and Dying' in here that'll just kill ya." Hard sell? Yes! Carlin was experiencing competitive pressure from a slew of new comedians making their mark in the waning days of the counter-culture movement led by Steve Martin.

Martin's debut album, *Let's Get Small* (Warner Bros.), went platinum with more than 1 million units sold. His appearances on the *Tonight Show* and *SNL* capped with his sold-out arena shows played a significant part in Martin's rise to the top of the comedy world—deservedly so. But that left George Carlin wanting in 1977. A plea to buy his record *On The Road* seems pathetic in retrospect but in keeping with Carlin's personal approach to his work and his fans. The libretto, as he calls it, was a printed transcript of the entire recording. Carlin was proud of his writing and less so of his performance.

On The Road was captured on tape on October 3, 1976, at the Dorothy Chandler Pavilion, annual site of the Academy Awards. It sounds like Carlin's before a full house, some 3,000 in attendance. The centerpiece is "Death and Dying," an abbreviated version of a longer routine also featured on Carlin's second HBO special. He covers it all here: suicide, funerals, murder, death row, and the two-minute warning, a humorous notion of secretly getting one from an angel. Carlin is at his philosophical best when he deconstructs dark subjects. To him, dying is not a taboo but a subject worthy of discussion in the microworld.

Another highlight are the tracks about kids written and performed from the perspective of a child. Carlin had a knack for imitating adult characters. This time, they come from a familiar place, his own childhood. At one point, he acts out the cliché of the single parent: "I have tried to be both a mother *and* father to you." The secret answer being "Go fuck yourself!," revealing Carlin's long-held reaction to his overbearing mother. The album closes with his ultimate microworld experience at the supermarket.

Carlin wasn't happy with the record, which he considered a disappointing retread. The decade of changing values, where he made his mark, was ending, and he knew it. So he took time off, cleaned up his drug dependency, and kept writing. As an artist, he was the best exponent of the 1960s; he was open to new ideas expressed in music and comedy. By the end of the decade, especially after Watergate, the ideals of American counterculture went mainstream. Notions of censorship were loosening up. Comedians were free, with some restrictions, to talk about politics, race, and equal rights for women. Carlin was, therefore, no longer a niche comedian. In the parlance of today, he needed a "reboot."

Carlin's 1981 studio album *A Place for My Stuff* includes a track called "Interview with Jesus." Asked why he "came back," Carlin, as Christ, says, "mostly nostalgia," and so it was for the comedian whose comeback mirrored the guy he was satirizing. In his memoir, Carlin is often critical of his work. He admits that the scripted material "really stunk" on this album, insisting that he had no "experience in the studio," which is ridiculous considering all of his formative years in broadcasting. The album put him back into the hearts and minds of his fans. "Stuff," "Fussy Eater," and Carlin's hammer throw on "Abortion" was just in time for the Reagan 1980s.

Carlin reached a new generation of comedians with his so-called concept album. One of them was San Francisco's Margaret Cho, who loved the precision of Carlin's routine "A Place for My Stuff." She was only thirteen years of age when she heard it, yet it struck her funny bone. The piece has a lot of merit. It's a comment on consumerism and Carlin's desire to use one word, "stuff," up to twenty-three times in one routine, which broke the rule of "three" most comics adhered to. He thought of it as an incantation casting an alliterative spell in the ear and on the page. (Carlin reproduced it in his book *Brain Droppings*.) The piece was a hit on the very first *Comic Relief* television charity special.

Carlin thought little of this record because he felt it came when he wasn't at his creative best. Many critics would beg to differ. It's the only Carlin album that features studio-produced routines besides live shows. Consequently, the uneven tracking affects the reliable flow of Carlin's ideas. Denny Dillon, the Tony-nominated actress, sits in the host chair on "Interview with Jesus" with Carlin playing the famous son of God. The live hunks come from the Sahara Hotel in Las Vegas, which is unusual because Carlin didn't find the Vegas crowd, his smart crowd, like the ones who went to his other shows. The title track and the heartwarming "Fussy Eater" routines leave a powerful impression.

He uses the tools with which he's comfortable, opening the record in National Public Radio (NPR) style: "This album has been made possible with grants from the following organizations: the institute

for Yahtzee theory . . . the international house of cream and sugar
. . . local twelve of the ball busters union." Then the album goes "live"
with Carlin's routine on "Stuff." It was Carlin's last audio project on
record. Subsequent releases were sound tracks to his television specials for HBO.

Carlin's enthusiasm for working his words in front of an audience
makes this album one of the most important in his canon. "Stuff"
became a signature routine for him, one of his microworld master-
pieces. Carlin is often remembered by a younger generation for this
routine as much as boomers recall his "Seven Words" piece. Carlin
wasn't necessarily conscious of his cross-generational work, but he
enjoyed the results in album sales and ticket sales to his shows. *A
Place for My Stuff* was nominated for a Grammy Award in 1983.

Carlin's enduring contributions to the art of the spoken word are,
to use a cliché, "legendary." He was nominated for a Grammy Award
seventeen times and won five times for Best Comedy Album. Spo-
tify, the streaming service, has more than 400 tracks by Carlin available to listeners around the world. His last album, *It's Bad for Ya*, is
still one of the best-selling records of his career.

Ten

THE CARLIN WARNING: SEVEN DIRTY WORDS AND THE FCC

*I*n Pasadena, California, lies the site of one of the most significant venues in George Carlin's career: the Ice House Comedy Club. It was here in October 1970 where Carlin debuted his original routine, "Seven Words You Can't Say on Television." The club appearance was barely a year after he'd been fired from the Frontier Hotel in Las Vegas for saying "shit" onstage. The Ice House appearance in front of a welcoming crowd was an epiphany for Carlin. "I knew I could do exactly what I wanted to do," he told *Gallery* magazine in an interview published the following spring.

Carlin worked on the "Seven Words" piece for months before bringing it into his act; it was time well spent. It's one of his best. But before he released the album *Class Clown*, Carlin experienced a legal intervention that was an eerie reminder of the trials of Lenny Bruce.

At the Milwaukee Summerfest on July 21, 1972, Carlin was booked to perform with musical guests Brewer & Shipley, the Seigal-Schwall Band, and Arlo Guthrie, who was the headliner. It was the fifth year of the music festival but Carlin's first and only appearance. On paper, it was a good gig. Carlin had released his second album, *FM & AM*, six months earlier to wide acclaim. He was performing regularly on the college circuit, including a recent appearance at Kent State University in Ohio, where, two years earlier, the National Guard killed

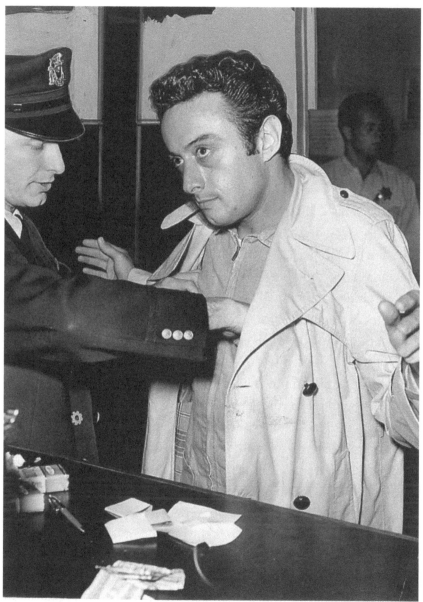

Lenny Bruce is arrested for obscenity at the Jazz Workshop, San Francisco, 1961. He was acquitted the following March at trial. WIKIMEDIA COMMONS

four students. So the Milwaukee audience of young people, *his* people, would have known him. They held the show at the lakefront amphitheater inside the main fairgrounds of Henry Maier Park. Carlin was scheduled for forty-five minutes.

Carlin's set that hot July evening included the new piece "Seven Words You Can't Say on Television." It had been part of his act for most of the spring, but where other audiences had laughed at Carlin's routine, here some festivalgoers complained, and the police were called. The story made the front page of the *Milwaukee Journal* on July 22, on the penultimate day of the festival. According to an Associated Press report, they arrested Carlin for "allegedly using profanity during a performance . . . Carlin was charged with disorderly conduct-profanity, and released after posting $150 bail." The article continues, "Henry Jordan, executive director of Summerfest and a former Green Bay Packer lineman, said Carlin's routine 'was definitely in bad taste. I was very disappointed.'" When the Milwaukee police arrested Carlin, they claimed to have "received numerous complaints from parents who were there with young children." In fact, an off-duty police officer by the name of Elmer Lenz was at the festival with his wife and child. He heard Carlin over the PA and called it in.

Carlin was first asked about this in the May 1973 issue of *Gallery* magazine. In the feature interview with Lawrence Linderman, Carlin says his microphone went dead during the performance, and a stagehand gave him another one. Then his wife Brenda, who toured with him in those days, came onstage and said, "You're going kind of long and there's trouble backstage with a police officer." Carlin finished his act and left the stage on the opposite side from where he entered. Exiting stage right, he went straight to his dressing room, giving him time to collect himself and wait for the police. They barged in and told the comedian that he'd "committed a verbal crime," as Carlin described it. The police continued to search his dressing room, possibly for contraband, but found nothing. In a photo taken by Mark Goff, who was on the scene, two burly members of Milwaukee's finest are escorting Carlin out of the park. He's wearing sandals, jeans, and a jean jacket over a tie-dyed T-shirt, typical of his look in those days. He's not wearing handcuffs, and he appears to be cooperating with the authorities. At the station, he was booked and photographed, with bail set at $150. Noting the odd timing of the malfunctioning microphone, journalist Dean Jensen wrote in the *Milwaukee Sentinel* (July 22, 1972) that Carlin's mic went dead *after* he said the seven words. Jensen writes, "After the crowd began shouting and clapping, another microphone was brought out to him."

Carlin tells Linderman that the state's attorney questioned the arresting officer, Elmer Lenz, at the hearing. They wanted to find out if the comedian actually committed the crime for which he was charged, "disorderly conduct." Even though Lenz said no, the city attorney's office refused to drop the charge. The case was eventually thrown out of court, says Carlin.

It wasn't as straightforward as that, according to James Sullivan in his biography of the comedian called *7 Dirty Words: The Life and Crimes of George Carlin* (2010). Sullivan goes into considerable detail about the arrest and the follow-up court case that eventually exonerated Carlin. He reports that when Carlin was arrested, he made his phone call to a local law firm, Coffey, Murray and Coffey, best known for defending civil rights cases. John Murray took the call and went down to police headquarters to speak to his new client. Sullivan says the police held Carlin for two hours and ran "a National Crime Information Center check on the comedian." (The NCIC is a database operated by the FBI.) Murray considered the move ridiculous because he believed that Carlin's crime didn't warrant that kind of scrutiny. After posting bond, Carlin, Murray, and his law partner William Coffey returned to the Pfister Hotel, where Carlin and his family were staying. In the early hours of July

22, they discussed their strategy. According to *Milwaukee Journal* staff reporter Barry Peterson, Summerfest paid Carlin his $3,000 fee. Carlin told the reporter, "The laws are here to protect me and so far they have protected me" (*Milwaukee Journal*, July 22, 1972).

Carlin fought the charges in deference to his lawyer's advice. Murray stated the comedian could waive his right to appear in court, so he kept his engagements and continued to tour. Six months later, following several adjournments, Carlin's trial finally came up on the docket in Wisconsin. The presiding judge was Raymond E. Gieringer. The prosecuting attorney was Ted Crockett, and John Murray represented Carlin. Two witnesses appeared for the prosecution. The first was a Catholic schoolteacher who was at the festival during Carlin's set. Murray questioned him about what he saw after he heard the seven words. The teacher said that the language he heard offended him but saw no disorderly conduct by anyone at the performance. "I saw people laughing," said the second witness, who was Assistant District Attorney Tom Schneider.

Fortunately for Carlin, the judge granted his lawyer permission to play back the routine on the *Class Clown* LP. It had just come out in September. According to James Sullivan, Judge Gieringer "laughed through the entire thing." Carlin was found not guilty of the charges, and the case was dismissed. Sullivan writes, "Carlin wasted no time exploiting the notoriety surrounding his arrest . . . giving the prosecuted words a group name . . . the Milwaukee Seven." According to a story published a week later in the *Milwaukee Journal* (July 28, 1972), Carlin appeared on the *Dick Cavett Show* walking onstage to the state's song, "On Wisconsin," telling Cavett that the words in the routine are "received well everywhere except Milwaukee."

This story has been told so many times that it has become embellished over the years, especially the part about Carlin's possession of cocaine. In the 1973 *Gallery* magazine interview, he says that Brenda asked him, before he left the stage, whether he had any drugs on him and, if so, to "give it to me." Carlin tells *Gallery*, "As it turned out, I wasn't carrying anything illegal, and I made it to the dressing room without too much trouble." Carlin may have said this at the time to protect himself and his wife, to prevent the police from hassling him on the road. Local narcotics officers who knew Lenny Bruce was an addict were often watching him.

Thirty years later, in *Last Words*, Carlin was more forthright about it, recalling that Brenda had tipped him off that the police were there to arrest him. In this telling, Carlin says that he inconveniently had cocaine stashed in his jacket at the time. Carlin said he left the stage on the opposite side where the police were and passed off the jacket to either to Corky (Siegel) or Jim (Schwall), members of the blues band who opened for him. "I'm clean and they're happy as hell. They have all my drugs" (*Last Words*).

Kelly Carlin, George's daughter, remembers the event as well in her autobiography *A Carlin Home Companion*. At the time, she was nine years of age. She writes, "Knowing that he was carrying drugs in his pocket—both grass and coke—my Mom thought fast, grabbed a glass of water, and walked out onto the stage. Dad, confused, took the water, and Mom whispered, 'exit stage left. The cops are here.'" All three exited to the dressing room, according to Kelly, where "Mom removed a rather large baggie of coke from her purse and stashed it in a bass drum, and Dad took out the joint and small vial of coke from his pockets and handed them to the promoter" (Charles Fain). Kelly panicked, as any kid would do when she saw her father arrested and "cuffed." She says her mother called the lawyer and paid the bail, $250.

While the telling of this story regarding Carlin's possession of drugs is inconsistent, the bottom line for the comedian was that the First Amendment didn't shield him in Milwaukee. One off-duty police officer who simply didn't enjoy hearing curse words squashed the comedian's right to free speech. Ironically, it was this kind of language Carlin believed he was free to express because he often heard it from law enforcement when he was a youth. Carlin loved words and didn't think the "seven words" on his list could harm anyone.

One of the best cuts on side 2 of *Occupation: Foole* is called "Filthy Words," an excellent eleven-minute dissertation on what Carlin regarded as a "sequel" to the "Seven Words" piece. The "Filthy Words" list is longer. It includes the original seven plus the words "fart," "turd," and "twat," forming the bulk of his lexical routine.

If you can't say them on television, can you say them on radio? On October 30, 1973, radio station WBAI, New York, played the track on a talk show called *Lunchpail.* The topic that day was about the double standards Americans have toward language and its taboos. The host of the program, Paul Gorman, broadcast "Filthy Words" to kick-start the discussion. He warned listeners in advance to tune out if they didn't want to hear it. One listener didn't heed the warning and was outraged. His name was John H. Douglas, and he filed a complaint to the FCC a month after the WBAI broadcast. He heard the program in his car with his son, who was around fifteen years of age. Douglas was an active member of the Morality in Media organization, a lobbying group devoted to the abolition of pornography and sex trafficking.

As author James Sullivan tells it, Douglas's complaint was the only one registered with the FCC, and he wrote to the FCC asking for WBAI's broadcast license to be suspended for "such blatant disregard for the public ownership of the airwaves" (*7 Dirty Words*). The complaint featured Douglas's biggest concern, that "any child could have been turning the dial, and tuned in to that garbage." Although Douglas did not have a transcript or audio recording of the broadcast, that would have been reason enough for the FCC to dismiss the complaint, the FCC followed up promptly with WBAI. (The FCC was looking for a test case regarding the First Amendment and their

mission to oversee the airwaves for what they considered objection-
able material.) The station didn't have a copy or transcript either and
referred the FCC to the original track on *Occupation: Foole*. In their
accompanying note, perhaps in their own defense, the station added
a strong letter of support for Carlin, stating that "because he is a
true artist in his field, we are of the opinion that the inclusion of the
material . . . contributed to a further understanding of the subject"
(taken from *7 Dirty Words*).

The FCC disagreed and called WBAI's owners, Pacifica Foundation, to Washington, D.C., for a hearing. Pacifica, it's important to
note, was under close watch by the regulator for past transgressions,
including a broadcast of Allen Ginsberg's reading of his poem *Howl*
back in the 1950s. One of its other stations, KPFA in San Francisco,
received a steady flow of complaints for its contentious programming and subject manner well into the 1960s. So the "Filthy Words"
case wasn't totally out of keeping with the FCC, which was cracking
down on obscenity complaints, although Pacifica probably felt tar-
geted. To be fair, it was the FCC's job to investigate anything that was
deemed by the public to be "a violation of the statute or FCC rules
regarding obscenity, indecency and profanity." First established in
1934, the commission's mandate changed over the years to include
regulation of content.

The FCC issued a warning to WBAI instead of a fine for broadcasting the Carlin track. As quoted in Sullivan's *7 Dirty Words*, "[The
commission] believes that such words are indecent . . . and have no
place on radio when children are in the audience." They stated that
the track was "patently obscene," according to the previous decision
from the U.S. Supreme Court. The FCC ruling, which was added to
WBAI's record, was made on February 21, 1975, eighteen months
after the station broadcast of "Filthy Words." On license renewal, the
station would be open to interventions that could affect the outcome
of upcoming hearings. It would give organizations like Morality in

Media the power to dispute Pacifica license renewals. To some critics, the verdict proved that the FCC was less concerned about the First Amendment and more concerned about safeguarding the ears of susceptible children who might be listening.

Pacifica and WBAI appealed the FCC's ruling to the U.S. Court of Appeals for the D.C. Circuit. The broadcaster felt hamstrung by the decision; Pacifica took pride in its alternative programming that engaged listeners by creating thoughtful debate about the purpose of language and freedom of speech. Two of the three appellate justices overturned the FCC's judgment, which set up another appeal, this time by the FCC, to the Supreme Court. Carlin did not take part in any of the constitutional arguments. He could stand back and watch the judicial system "work." He did, however, take part in a community event for the WBAI legal defense fund.

In the case of *FCC v. Pacifica Foundation*, the Supreme Court ruled five to four in favor of the commission. The Court considered the broadcast of "Filthy Words" indecent but not obscene yet subject to restriction, as written by Justice Stevens. They also ruled that the FCC could fine any station for broadcasting, in their opinion, any material harmful to children. The Court passed the decision on July 3, 1978, roughly five years after the WBAI broadcast. The FCC could now legally fine, censure, or restrict any media it licensed for broadcasting so-called dirty words.

A transcript of the "Filthy Words" track from the album was added to the record of the Supreme Court. It included the all-important description after every joke: "frequent laughter from the audience." Reading the complete transcript, it's easy to conclude that Justice Brennan, who wrote the dissenting opinion, got Carlin's joke and that Justice Stevens, who represented the majority, didn't.

Carlin held a press conference the day they released the decision, July 4, 1978. He held firm to his belief that the First Amendment "didn't allow" for an appointed board to decide what could or could not be said. The night after the Supreme Court decision, Carlin hosted the *Tonight Show*, and Ed McMahon asked him about it. "The words are crude . . . but whether they should be illegal; whether or not we should be enjoined from using them . . . I don't agree, personally. That's why they call it an 'opinion.'" WBAI posted a sign on their studio door: "Remember the Carlin Warning!"

To this day, the story—the Supreme Court ruling and the discussion about Carlin's monologue—continues. Scott Bomboy, the editor in chief of Constitutioncenter.org, weighs in on the case and its impact on constitutional law. The case came up during a hearing in 2012 when the FCC wanted to fine FOX and ABC "for what it deemed as offensive content." Bomboy refers to the 1978 verdict, calling it "a decision that still holds sway over the use of indecent and obscene language on television, and in a new era of mass communications." In the same article, the late Justice Ruth Bader Ginsburg

WBAI, New York. ROB VINCENT / WIKIMEDIA COMMONS

said that the Pacifica decision was "wrong when it was issued" and was worthy of "reconsideration" (July 3, 2021).

Carlin, free to sit back and let the legal cards fall where they may, was proud that they identified him with the debate. He was content knowing that the only way the justices could hear the evidence back in 1978 was by listening to the record or reading a transcript of his engrossing piece "Filthy Words."

In a related story, the Library of Congress officially added the LP *Class Clown* to the National Recording Registry for Preservation in 2015.

Eleven

THE HBO LIFELINE

"*H*BO saved me," declared George Carlin, "and that has kept me in front of a mass audience without censorship, not just fuck, shit and piss. I mean ideas that would not be welcome on commercial enterprise television" (Televisionacademy.com). When Carlin's album sales were declining in the late 1970s, HBO was a worthy media substitute. Carlin took advantage of an opportunity to perform *his* way on a media platform with which he was most familiar. He would end up creating fourteen specials for HBO, some of the most important and timeless programs in the history of television. HBO was his redeemer.

When Carlin was breaking out as a solo performer in 1965, the City of New York granted an ambitious entrepreneur by the name of Charles Dolan a license to create and implement a cable television system in Lower Manhattan. He named the company Manhattan Cable, and it went live in September 1966. The service was modest at first, as Dolan's company hooked up every hotel and apartment building in the area with Teleguide, an information service channel that featured local tourism news in a scrolling format. Antenna received all television signals, be it the traditional rabbit ears on top of your set or as connected to a rooftop tower that picked up the transmissions of the big three networks, ABC, CBS, and NBC. If you had the right equipment, you could also receive channels on the UHF (ultrahigh frequency) airwaves. Cable's enormous advantage was that it offered customers a strong and consistent signal regardless of the weather. But it was very expensive to hook up every household.

Charles Dolan persevered, even though his company, renamed Sterling Communications, was losing money. The expense of running cable underneath the city and into televisions around New York could run up to $300,000 per mile. Dolan went to Time-Life Inc. and sold them a quarter share of the company to stay afloat. Over the short term, their investment would lift Dolan's notion of a commercial-free channel with subscribers into a stronger business opportunity—even better if it offered movies licensed from Hollywood in their original, unedited presentations.

In the summer of 1971, after getting approval from the FCC to operate a cable TV system, Dolan came up with the Green Channel, a movie and sports format for a monthly fee, just like a magazine or newspaper subscription. Pay television, as it came to be called, arrived with a splash. With the help of Time-Life Inc., whose subscription database was huge, a massive mail campaign spread the word. In November, Dolan's Sterling Communications made a licensing deal with the motion picture industry to pay a flat rate for TV broadcast rights. Besides sports, Dolan now had the content to get programming to his subscribers, but it was still a hard sell. It accustomed customers to getting their TV shows for free.

HBO officially launched a year later on November 8, 1972, with an NHL hockey game between the Vancouver Canucks and the New York Rangers. HBO had a modest 365 subscribers at a fee of $6 per month. Programming on the channel ran from 7 p.m. to midnight daily. By February 1973, subscriptions increased to 4,000, so things were looking up for the fledgling service.

As the company grew, HBO launched a satellite in 1975 to send their feed to cable companies nationally. They were now in a financial position to produce original programming, besides licensing sports events and movies. On December 31, 1975, the first HBO comedy special with Robert Klein debuted. Klein did another nine over his illustrious thirty-year career. *An Evening with Robert Klein* was a critical success for both HBO and the comedian. It led to the production of more "specials" under the series title *On Location.*

By 1977, George Carlin was no longer enjoying the massive success he generated only five years earlier with the release of his comedy albums on Little David. The first three had gone gold (500,000 copies sold), and he was doing well in 1973. He was earning more than $1 million a year doing concerts, club dates, and TV appearances. It was a fruitful time, but it didn't last forever because the competition for original comedy was getting brisk. Steve Martin, Robert Klein, Robin Williams, and Richard Pryor had all released their own successful albums by booting the class clown into the corridor. Undeterred, Carlin worked harder.

HBO sent him a "lifeline," as he told Charlie Rose in 1996. It was uncensored, unexpurgated, and free of producer interference, offering the competitive comedian a perfect solution. With HBO backing him, Carlin reached a mass audience with his latest ideas, just like an album, in a one-hour TV show.

Michael Fuchs was the first director of programming for HBO. Born in Bronx in 1946, he was cynical about the political climate in the post-Watergate mid-1970s. He believed comedians were more thoughtful, provocative, and relevant, and he wanted HBO to produce programs featuring their point of view. He told Joel Fleming, a cable TV executive, "Very early on I wanted us to be more candid, more open, more fresh, more experimental, more daring than the networks, who to me, were homogenized; it was canned entertainment, it had no guts" (Cablecenter.org, June 3, 1999).

In *7 Dirty Words*, author James Sullivan does a good job explaining the legal and disclaimer issues faced by HBO before Carlin's first special was broadcast. Management worried about the ramifications of Carlin's act and his potential use of the seven words you can never say on television. The FCC case before the Supreme Court against WBAI was months away from a hearing, but the D.C. Court of Appeals reversed the FCC decision to fine WBAI just as Carlin and HBO were going into production. Still, HBO wasn't interested in bringing the ire of the FCC on their back. They carried on with a recording date scheduled for March 5, 1977, at the University of Southern California. They set the broadcast date for Good Friday, April 8. Michael Fuchs said it was "intentional."

Marty Callner, who had directed the Robert Klein special two years earlier, was assigned to direct Carlin's first and second specials for HBO. Callner's résumé would grow to include a long list of stand-up comedy specials for HBO, including Robin Williams's first special *Off the Wall* (1978), Jerry Seinfeld's *I'm Telling You for the Last Time* (1998), and Will Ferrell's *You're Welcome America: A Final Night with George W. Bush* (2009). Callner remembers his work with Carlin, his wife Brenda, and Artie Warner, Carlin's manager at the time. On a Reddit post in January 2021, with an image of all four taken in Phoenix, Callner says, "He [Carlin] was one of my first assignments at HBO, and we hit it off immediately. I directed his first ever stand-up comedy special for television, which included the seven words you can't say on television . . . I almost got fired from HBO for insisting on the bit staying in the show. Alas, the smarter minds prevailed. I directed his second special, the infamous show in the round from Phoenix. From there, we were like family . . . George is the smartest person I've ever known, by far. His ability to take what we all feel, and put it into timeless comedy, is a gift unmatched" (Reddit .com/r/GeorgeCarlin). It's hard to believe Callner "was almost fired" for standing firm on the censoring of the "Seven Words" routine because it contradicts HBO's noneditorial involvement in their comedy specials. Nevertheless, HBO exercised caution.

On Location opens with a special introduction by Shana Alexander, who was a commentator on *60 Minutes*, the long-serving TV newsmagazine produced by CBS. It's a weird opening as Alexander welcomes us to the broadcast with high praise for Carlin as an artist. She compares his use of vulgar language to Aristophanes, Chaucer, and Shakespeare. She warns us that this special "contains language you hear every day on the street though rarely on TV," as if hearing this language on TV is worse than hearing it on the street. HBO was taking no chances because they were playing defense against the FCC, so they could say, in all honesty, that if anyone watching was offended, they were forewarned and forearmed (to laugh).

As the show finally begins, they interview briefly Carlin about some of his influences, naming the Marx Brothers, Danny Kaye, and Lenny Bruce. Then he's asked a poignant question: "What are the most dramatic ways you are forced to alter your performances for television?" He says he can "suspend" use of the seven words while getting his ideas across. Then he goes into a censorship story about an appearance on the *Ed Sullivan Show* when the producers asked him to pick one of two controversial jokes for the broadcast back in 1971. He also makes a casual but important remark: "You don't go in there to try to change their system, usually. You go in there to fit within it, for your own narrow purposes."

Carlin's first HBO special is one continuous performance. He's comfortable and energized by a friendly audience, mostly college age. At one point, his microphone fails and he has to replace it, which makes the performance feel authentic (unedited) for the viewer at home. (He may have had flashbacks to the Milwaukee Summerfest in 1972!) Highlights include his response to a groan elicited by one of his jokes—"I have a theory about why people moan at certain jokes . . . envy"—and his dogs and cats routines, complete with facial expressions. His words pour out of his movements. But the ninety-minute show blossoms during the last half hour when Carlin goes into airlines and their "perversion of language" and the confusing use of three words: "flammable, non-flammable, and inflammable."

Just as Carlin leads us into his next hunk featuring the seven words, HBO freezes the frame. A warning comes up asking viewers to "consider whether you wish to continue viewing" just in case you can't handle his "controversial language." Some viewers must have seen the warning as an invitation to keep watching.

After working language ambiguities into his act for the past five years, Carlin was merging the ideas from "Seven Words" (1972) and "Filthy Words" (1973) into a single routine. In this HBO version, he softens it with fart jokes, yet we're witnessing a change in Carlin's presentation. He's thinking on his feet, moving from one idea to the next, often pausing for dramatic effect. It's a bit of a ruse; he knows exactly what he wants to say because he has memorized the routine and paced it to get laughs every twenty seconds (a formula Lenny Bruce standardized), and it worked. The show was a hit for HBO and a boost to Carlin's morale.

Twelve months later, Carlin entered the hospital for heart trouble. He was driving his daughter Kelly to school and suffered what they later diagnosed as myocardial infarction. Carlin had tightness in his jaw, left arm, and upper back but no pain in his chest. They discharged him after two days and told him to rest, but the ever-energetic comedian maintained his touring schedule around the United States, often landing in Las Vegas for extended runs. Work was his way of recovering.

The Celebrity Star Theater in Phoenix was the site of Carlin's second HBO special, *George Carlin Again!* The venue opened in 1964 with a production of *South Pacific*, which must have been a choreographer's worst nightmare since this was theater in the round: an open stage with no curtain surrounded by 2,650 seats. But on July 23, 1978, it was Carlin's stage in front of a sold-out house. The video looks edited in places, but the performance rolls along as Carlin works his material in front of another receptive audience. (This was his third of several performances in the theater that week.) He does a remarkable routine about "Time" and all its variables in the English language, putting forth his thoughtful point with assurance that "there's no time, we made it up. It's a man-made invention: time," brilliantly concluding that "sometimes we know *where* we are. But we don't really know *when* we are."

In the middle of his set, someone tosses him a bottle of Visine eyedrops, to which he replies, "Do they look that red?" Then someone tosses him a joint, to which he replies, "Okay, now I need it" to a huge response from the audience. Carlin's love of marijuana was an essential part of his appeal; at his Toronto performance in 1982, you had to peer through the cannabis smoke just to see him onstage.

In a nostalgic turn, Carlin launches into his favorite pot smoker, Al Sleet, "by request," he says. Then comes his brilliant routine on death: "If you think being sick is no fun, dying is really a pain in the ass. . . . Where do we go? . . . you go where you want to go . . . because it's on the schedule." Carlin's advice is to "go big" when you're about to die by taking your last two minutes of life with a rousing, eloquent, "bring it to the rafters" speech, concluding, "if this is not the truth, may *God strike me dead!*"

Carlin ends with "Filthy Words," an identical performance from the first special in 1977. His commitment never wavers as he dedicates the last few minutes to the meaning of "fuck" and its hundreds of combinations. Carlin's extraordinary performance on this special is in the pocket, as they say in music. He's energized by every word, phrase, and movement, all fueled by steady laughter. He was forty-one years of age and, seemingly, at the top of his game.

Between 1978 and 1981, Carlin had a new list of personal crises with which to contend. He had one heart attack, unpaid back taxes, no recording contract, fewer TV appearances, and a failed movie project, *The Illustrated George Carlin*. His wife Brenda was recovering from alcohol abuse. His daughter Kelly was struggling to find her direction in life by relying on pot, cocaine, and poor relationships with men to resolve it. Although Carlin had kicked cocaine, the residual effects pushed him into heavy drinking and reckless behavior. On July 7, 1981, while on the road from Toronto to Dayton, Carlin left Canada after a gig and drove to Ohio. He picked up some beer and proceeded to drink and drive. By some miracle of fate, just outside Dayton, he survived a car crash into a utility pole, suffering a broken nose and cuts to his face. A plastic surgeon was on duty in the St. Elizabeth Medical Center emergency room. As his daughter later described it, "[The doctor] put his face back together almost as good as new. He got lucky" (*A Carlin Home Companion*).

Carlin's financial trouble was a combination of negligence and procrastination. In 1976, he hired Monte Kay, producer of his Little David records, to manage his affairs. Kay hired an accounting firm called Brown-Kraft & Co. to look after Carlin's finances. Brown and Kraft had some high-end Hollywood clients, including actor Marlon Brando. Carlin, however, ignored any correspondence from the company, which sent him monthly statements. It's not known why he stopped opening their mail (he says little about it in his memoir), but it would eventually catch up with him down the road: $1 million in unpaid taxes. Why Brown and Kraft and Monte Kay didn't insist that Carlin deal with it is unknown. Carlin fell into the habit of putting it off while taking care of the health of his family, all the while pursuing a career that had slowed artistically and commercially. He needed another lifeline.

In the liner notes of the Little David box set, released in 1999, author Michael Krugman says that Carlin's use of cocaine distorted his judgment. Carlin admits it in his memoir that the "cocaine years," as he often called them, yielded a few albums and TV appearances, but the material, in his opinion, wasn't as good. He decided it was time for some introspection, and you can hear it in his work, especially *On The Road*, released in April 1977. Carlin's remarkable skill of writing and performing material that channeled his personal conflicts speaks to his strengths as an artist. What came easily for him in 1970 when he emerged with a new look and plan was now falling apart. The poet had the words but not the means to save himself. This time, he needed help, and he got it from Jerry Hamza.

In his memoir, Carlin said that Jerry Hamza played an important and influential role in his life and career. Hamza was born in Rochester, New York, son of a country music promoter and born fly fisher. In 1977, he worked for his father, who asked him to book Carlin for some shows in Rochester and Syracuse since Carlin had successful concerts in Ohio. He knew little about the comedian, but after a four sold-out shows in Syracuse, he knew Carlin was a hit with audiences. When Hamza went backstage to meet him for the first time, he said a reporter for the local newspaper was interested in an interview. Carlin replied, "Why? Is it my birthday?" The pair hit it off, and Hamza started working for Carlin as his concert promoter and booking agent. By 1980, he became his full-time manager. He respected Carlin's work ethic and dedication to his craft. His plan to go "hot" and "big" with Carlin's career engaged the comedian's imagination. Hamza was focused and thoughtful, and he arrived at a critical point in Carlin's life. His commitment to excellence and his seriousness as a manager impressed Carlin. Hamza even moved his family from Rochester to Los Angeles to prove it. It was the beginning of a beautiful friendship.

Hamza's first task was to get Carlin's financial house in order. He replaced Brown-Kraft & Co. with his trusted accountants, Bonadio-Insero (known today as Insero & Co.). Brown-Kraft was based in Los Angeles, where the Internal Revenue Service held tight scrutiny of the Hollywood elite. Hamza was worried that news of Carlin's financial issues would leak and affect his plan for the comedian, which included a new album and more TV appearances. (This wasn't tax avoidance as much as avoiding bad press.)

Carlin's profile cooled a little, and Hamza wanted him to come back strong. By hiring a new accounting firm to handle Carlin's taxes, Hamza could focus on getting Carlin back into writing and performing without distractions. Carlin was a willing client, ready to leave the messed-up cocaine years behind.

The first thing Hamza did was set up a new contract with Atlantic Records. He believed Carlin needed to release a new album and let the world know that he was back and better than ever. The record deal wasn't lucrative because Carlin's album sales declined after the release of *An Evening with Wally Londo* and its follow-up *On the Road*. The sales figures did not impress the brass. Nevertheless, the $100,000 advance from Atlantic provided enough incentive for Carlin to write and produce what he called a concept album, *A Place for My Stuff*.

Hamza also supported Carlin's movie project *The Illustrated George Carlin*, a semibiographical/performance/animated film inspired by Richard Pryor's *In Concert* movie released in 1979. Carlin invested a lot of time and money into the film, seeking backers from Toronto no less. But he failed to get the project off the ground. Nobody seemed to be interested in him or his work anymore despite a growing interest in comedy. That said, audiences were looking away from the guy who made stand-up a legitimate art form by the end of the decade. Carlin was out of fashion, just like lava lamps, discos, and wide lapels on leisure suits.

Jerry Hamza played the long game. He got Carlin a *Playboy* magazine feature interview published in the January 1982 issue. By this time, *Playboy* had become the go-to publication for an older, male demographic. Unlike their centerfolds, they took their monthly interview subjects earnestly by printing long, in-depth conversations. Carlin's interview was extensive. The reporter, Sam Merrill, met with Carlin seven times over two weeks, gathering fifteen hours' worth of questions and answers on tape. Carlin talks about his entire life, admitting that the cocaine years hurt him. He was regrouping, considering his options, and looking ahead for better, more creative days in his life. After the issue of *Playboy* was released, Hamza secured New York's prestigious Carnegie Hall for Carlin's next HBO special, a monumental venue for an equally monumental career move.

Despite the bright future before him, Carlin suffered another heart attack in May 1982 during a Mets–Dodgers game in Los Angeles. He was with Hamza and barely made it to hospital but for the excellent

Carlin at Carnegie Hall. PHOTOFEST

skill of their driver, John Battiste, who took Carlin to Saint John's in Santa Monica. There they gave him a new blood clot medication called streptokinase, specifically used for heart patients in cardiac arrest. It worked until he had an operation in Atlanta in July. Carlin joked about it in his shows, comparing his score to Richard Pryor, who suffered a heart attack in 1977. Carlin was up three to two.

On October 12, 1982, Carlin returned to the stage in a big way: a performance at Carnegie Hall. The theater was famous for some of the most important music concerts in history, including Benny Goodman in 1938 with Carlin's favorite drummer, Gene Krupa. It was also the site of Lenny Bruce's legendary show on a cold February night in 1961. To say that it was special for Carlin would be an understatement. He was about to make a comeback. He had new material and a new look, dropping the tie-dyed T-shirts and jeans for a sweater and slacks à la Mort Sahl. He was forty-five and thin and had no ponytail and a little gray in the beard yet was ready to entertain, break the rules, and philosophize.

Carlin didn't like the venue. "Carnegie Hall is a cold place . . . not a good room to hear your laughs," he said years later in his interview on Television.academy.com in 2007. Still, he knew how to work a room. This time, he stood on an enormous rug as part of a dressed stage with chairs piled behind him like a set out of an Ionesco play.

The bulk of the performance features material from 1981, specifically his masterwork "Fussy Eater" and his commentary on the popular greeting "have a nice day." These bits first appeared on the *A Place for My Stuff* album, but the TV versions are much more satisfying because we get Carlin's facial expressions. It may have been six months since his last concert performance, as he admits, but he's strong, less manic than the previous two HBO specials. His hunk "Dogs & Cats #2" is beautifully written. Carlin corners the dog story niche with every known activity, from dog farts to how a dog understands time (as "forever") and why the animal reacts in a big way when you come home. He segues to cats when he says that unlike dogs, cats "don't have eyebrows." He spoke from personal experience because pets were a part of Carlin's life at home. The last part of his set is dedicated specifically to words that sound dirty "if you gave them a little help, such as pussyfoot and cocktails." The closer is a fully expanded version of "Dirty Words" featuring a prop: a printed scroll of some 200 words and phrases considered obscene, from which he reads as the credits roll.

Despite his energy, solid timing, and delivery, Carlin wasn't happy with his performance. He sulked about it, believing that he had missed an opportunity to come back even bigger after a six-month absence. His wife Brenda, who produced the show, agreed, but the HBO subscribers did not. When the show was broadcast four months later, it was a smash, helping relaunch Carlin into the stand-up "sweepstakes" featuring Steve Martin, Richard Pryor, Robin Williams, and Eddie Murphy. *Carlin at Carnegie!* marked an important phase for Carlin's long-term commitment to HBO on a biennial basis. Every two years, Carlin would write and record a new HBO special. The new deal restored his confidence. He worked hard to prepare new material for every succeeding special until 2008.

The Carnegie gig was also an important turning point in the relationship between Carlin and his mother. It took Mary a long time to accept the ideas her son expressed onstage. She attended the performance and was taken aback by his commentary on all the things she held dear, namely, religion and respect for the world of business. She still wanted George to be that man of respectability her husband never was, clinging to her unreasonable expectations. Mary was Carlin's toughest critic. She could accept him as a six-year-old mimic but was uneasy with him as an adult with a sharp tongue. Eventually, she came around after meeting up with two nuns from Corpus Christi Church. One day, they met Mary on the street and affirmed that her hilarious son was disarming the power of obscene words as a service to humanity. It was all she needed to hear, two fans in vestments granting her son absolution.

Eighteen months after Carlin's successful return to the concert stage, he returned to the college crowd with his fourth HBO special, *Carlin on Campus*. Recorded at the Wadsworth Theater at the University of California, Los Angeles, over two days in 1984, it also portioned the special out on the album.

Carlin opens the program with a nostalgic trip down memory lane, at least for him, a visit with the class clown re-created in a tiny classroom. He's expelled when the teacher (Carlin wearing a nun's habit) says, "I'm glad she kicked me out. I didn't want to be in there, anyway." He then proceeds to the stage, whose weird *Twilight Zone* minimalist design features a pyramid on stage right and a large orb on stage left. The floor is bare except for a series of white stripes creating a false depth of field. A few illustrated clouds float in the background. After he warms up the crowd, he gets right to the religious material with "The Prayer," dedicated to the separation of church and state. "Our Father who art in heaven, and to the Republic in which it stands . . . ," a clever merger of the Lord's Prayer and the Pledge of Allegiance. He then launches into a fast-paced version of "A Place for My Stuff." To punch up the special, animated sequences called "Drawing on My Mind" are included that Carlin wrote and narrated. Kurtz & Friends, founded by Bob Kurtz, whose work was most familiar to viewers of *Sesame Street* in the early 1970s, created these vignettes.

Carlin's well-written hunk on cars and driving is definitive microworld. He performs the entire piece seated, a rarity for the man who loved to walk the stage back and forth. Yet we forget he's stationary because he's having so much fun driving an imaginary car. Carlin's take is edgy; what starts out as a Sunday drive in the country turns into road rage.

He closes the show with a familiar routine going back to 1975, "Baseball and Football," because, as he says, "they are such a part of our lives and yet they're so different." Unlike his *SNL* monologue, this version is fully realized as Carlin uses every phrase in the military jargon of football to the utmost, contrasting the rough sport to the pastoral nature of baseball. After the performance ends, in a quiet afterword, he closes the special at the piano playing his instrumental composition "Armadillo Blues" underneath the credits. (Carlin took piano lessons when he was a kid.)

Carlin on Campus is a solid piece of television from start to finish. The animated features matched Carlin's more irreverent humor, particularly the "Rosary Monster," illustrated as a huge green beast gobbling up a Catholic rosary until it's cross-eyed. The staged opening and closing segments bookend Carlin's live show. He's emboldened on his fourth special, marking his confident return. Jerry Hamza was right: go big or stay home.

Carlin was on a roll. In 1984, he and Jerry Hamza formed a new production company to oversee all of his future work. Cablestuff Productions was the name, and his wife Brenda and daughter Kelly staffed it in a genuine family-run business. They set up offices in Brentwood, California, and soon started work on a TV pilot for a potential HBO series. The show was *Apt. 2C*, and Carlin had full creative control. He hired writers to help him build a legit television series. It was a risky and expensive proposition, but HBO was supportive of the pilot and its creator. *Apt. 2C* was recorded before a studio audience at the A&M Studios on La Brea Boulevard in Los Angeles. This was the site of Charlie Chaplin's movie studios in the 1920s, now home to the Jim Henson Company.

Despite the good Chaplin karma, the well-intentioned *Apt. 2C* is caustic, confused, and only occasionally funny. Yet the pilot took some creative risks. Carlin breaks the fourth wall and talks about his life as a writer. He doesn't really get any writing done because his kooky neighbors keep interrupting him. Most of the gags are exten-sions of Carlin's stand-up routine interspersed with quirky charac-ters that drop by every couple of minutes. A lot of time, money, and effort went into this pilot; the mock apartment set design is beauti-ful, and the commitment to character by the actors is solid, but there isn't anything likable about them. The notable appearances of Bobcat Goldthwait and Kelly Carlin can't save the piece either. Goldthwait's over-the-top caffeine-laced character comes on too strong, and while daughter Kelly's portrayal of a Girl Scout with a difference is funny, there's no reason for her character to return after she crushes her box of cookies when George says they're "too firm to eat."

Apt. 2C as a concept has some merit if we're led to believe that the audience was getting a little closer to learning how Carlin came up with his material, but it doesn't. He's playing a version of himself as the outsider in a crazy world of crazy people, which is a good premise, but everybody is trying too hard to make an impression. In the end, we're no closer to Carlin the artist than we were at the beginning. As a transitional work, *Apt. 2C* reveals Carlin's growth as an actor and his desire to experiment with different ideas.

HBO preferred his stand-up shows and rejected the pilot. Carlin pressed on by visiting *SNL*. Dick Ebersol, who took over temporarily for Lorne Michaels, who left NBC, invited him back. This episode of *SNL*, broadcast on November 10, 1984, was an important shift in Carlin's participation in the show. Back in 1975 when he hosted the debut program, Carlin was in a post-cocaine comedown. He didn't feel up to doing any sketches, and he wanted to do a few routines in between the music and sketch elements. Nine years later, sober, motivated, and more comfortable "acting," Carlin takes part fully, including a familiar bit as the newsman, anchoring *Saturday Night News* as it was called.

"We started [1984] with Orwell and ended up with Falwell," says Carlin on his opening monologue, harkening back to his first appearance when he got a slap on the wrists for talking trash about God. Carlin does his "prayer" from *Carlin on Campus* to huge applause. Years after they prosecuted Lenny Bruce for criticizing Catholicism, religious material was getting into mainstream comedy by the mid-1980s, and *SNL* cornered the market by its tenth season. Father Guido Sarducci, played by Don Novello, appeared first in 1978. His refined satire of the Catholic Church and its rituals never intended to offend, only entertain. He was successful for years, poking fun at the Vatican and its institutions. Besides his guest appearances on *Late Night* with David Letterman, Novello appeared on *SNL* thirty-one times as his version of the hippy-dippy priest.

In his first sketch, a parody of the *Joe Franklin Show*, a local New York talk show, Carlin plays the role of Dan, a firefighter seated between Martin Short's character Jackie Rogers Jr. and Senor Cosa, a ventriloquist played by Christopher Guest. Billy Crystal plays Joe Franklin. Of this, Carlin recalls in his memoir that Short was complimentary about his work on the sketch, while Crystal was less so. But for Carlin, it was enough for him to pursue acting with more determination, leading to a role in Arthur Hiller's comedy *Outrageous Fortune*, released in 1985. His confident appearance on *SNL* wasn't the drudgery it was in 1975.

In 1986, Carlin returned to the Beverly Theater in Los Angeles for his next HBO special. This time, a new director, Rocco Urbisci, joined the production team for this and the next nine programs for HBO. It was a professional relationship that went back to 1971 when Urbisci met Carlin on the *Tonight Show*. Urbisci had just arrived in Los Angeles pursuing a career in show business as a writer. When he met Carlin, he pitched an idea for a satire called *Captain Catholic*, a religious superhero with a cape in Vatican colors who helps people but is really interested in making money. Carlin was amused by the idea and asked Urbisci to stay in touch. Urbisci, meanwhile, carved out a career as a TV producer, getting a job with the *Midnight Special*, the late-night music program that was broadcast Friday nights on NBC after the *Tonight Show*. Carlin appeared as a guest in 1973 and a year later hosted the *Midnight Special* in May. The program featured Buffy Sainte-Marie, Waylon Jennings, and the Dramatics, part of the series' wide-ranging musical repertoire. Carlin's impressive work as host led him to *SNL* when it debuted.

Urbisci met up with Carlin again after his show in the Wadsworth Theater in 1984, and to his surprise, Carlin asked him to direct his next HBO special, *Playin' with Your Head*. They gave Urbisci free reign to write and direct an inventive opening, and he does so with a short black-and-white drama called *The Envelope*. It's a parody of the film noir pictures Warner Bros. produced in the 1940s. For this short, Carlin plays the part of Mike Holder, a writer whose job is to prepare another script for HBO. Three thugs, led by actor Vic Tayback, want the envelope with the new material in Carlin's possession. He escapes out the back window, and they chase him. Then the trio confronts Carlin backstage at the theater, like a pack of G-men. Carlin replies, "You just don't get it, do you? It's over for you guys. Besides, you wouldn't know what to do with this [holding the envelope]." Carlin walks through a door and enters the stage in front of an enthusiastic audience, holding the precious envelope. This was Carlin's subtle jab at censorship.

Playin' with Your Head is about logic and how we communicate. Carlin starts the show with his first-rate "Hello and Goodbye," dedicated to the language of greetings and departures. He then satirizes charities by making up his own, including "battered plants," a hunk about the psychological implications of hanging plants. Carlin's presence and confidence in his new material is extraordinary. He was moving to a new plateau of ideas regarding the little world and the things we have in common, like what we do when we lose things. "Where do things go when they're lost? I think there's a big pile of things somewhere . . . and where is the pile? In heaven, of course

. . . that's the first thing that happens when you get to heaven. They give you everything you ever lost." He concludes, "That's the whole meaning of heaven . . . with a special room for all the balloons that were lost." *Playin' with Your Head* was nominated for a Grammy Award in 1987.

Carlin was maturing as a comedian. Gone were the dog and cat jokes, the trouble with airlines, and unacceptable behavior at the grocery store. He was finally coming out of his creative stupor in 1986 with original works based on his newfound learning. Carlin was usually in a state of continuous self-education beyond the daily news. During the Reagan years, he dived into alternative publications such as *Mother Jones* magazine and the anticorporate periodical *In These Times*. He wanted to enrich and expand his political thinking and roll it into his work. As an informed comedian, he could comment on the macroworld and the broader topics of racism and the struggles of class, ideas he first learned from Jack Burns. The more he read, the more he disdained liberal thinkers who exhibited "knee-jerk reactions to certain issues" (*Last Words*). Carlin was taking notes to become, like Frank Zappa, the equal opportunity offender. He didn't like groupthink. He wanted to remove himself from the freak show and focus on the big picture as an emerging philosopher.

If there was one audience Carlin loved the most during the 1980s, it was in New Jersey. The West Coast audiences were wonderful but too soft, according to the comedian, who felt they were less attentive to his emotionally charged shows. The raucous East Coast fans jammed the Park Theater in Union City for Carlin's sixth HBO special, *What Am I Doing in New Jersey?*, in March 1988. They were ready to be entertained. This time, Carlin took a risk of performing the show as a live broadcast, with no safety net and no room for technical errors. Besides, after two terms under Reagan, Carlin was armed to go to the breach and drill into the political cracks of the American system and fight with a louder, more critical voice.

What Am I Doing in New Jersey? opens with a short vignette that sees Carlin hailing a cab and riding through the streets of New York. When Carlin asks the driver, played by Carlin's friend Bob Altman, to take him to New Jersey, the cabbie replies, "Is there any way you can get out of it?" Carlin says, "No, I don't think so. It has something to do with Original Sin." The cabbie agrees to drive him from the Hotel Dorset to Union City via the Holland Tunnel to New Jersey.

When he arrives, Carlin takes the stage, which is elaborately dressed with a high fence behind him, empty oil cans, skids, and a mural of a factory matching the rough-and-tumble neighborhood in which he's situated. The stage is industrial, earthy, and gritty, reflecting the streetwise sensibility that was planted in Carlin as a youth. He was fifty years of age, annoyed with the outgoing president and all the political and social havoc he wreaked in America. This performance, two years in the making, merged his sense of injustice with a higher political sensibility.

Carlin specifically developed his potent mix of commentary for this audience with the routine "Reagan's Gang, Church People and American Values." For nearly twelve minutes, he takes the time to focus the piece on the contradiction between Reagan's law-and-order message and the fact that a couple hundred different people in the administration had been "fired or arrested or prosecuted or jailed for violating the ethics code" the administration so proudly sold as its first priority. As Carlin summarizes, "They want to put street criminals in jail to make life safer for the business criminals." Carlin is visibly angry over the absurdity of First Amendment violations, calling out the FCC on its unaccountable power to censor free speech. And he puts in a harsh word about the power of the Religious Right. He's disappointed in the promise of a system of equal rights for all its citizens that favors only the wealthy one-percenters.

The last time Carlin voted was the 1980 federal election. He took his vote and his stake in democracy out of the game, freeing himself from participating in what he considered another American false-hood. Now he could stand back and observe and note and refine his objections into his act, often with brilliant results. "It's a strange culture," says Carlin, "where they think about banning toy guns and they're gonna keep the fucking real ones!" This HBO special is a well-crafted gateway to his next level: artist as philosopher. The jokes had to delve into the human psyche.

Carlin was a big fan of Sam Kinison, the smart, caustic comedian whose high-pitched vocal wail distinguished his act from the quieter performers in comedy like Tim Allen or Jerry Seinfeld. Carlin felt he had to stand out from the crowded, noisy culture by getting louder and more abrasive in his delivery. His sixth special reflects Carlin's love for Kinison's style and how effective he, too, could be with a boisterous presentation. For the better part of forty-five minutes, Carlin plays the angry comic, and he's dazzling. In her memoir, daughter Kelly says that her father "found new energy and intensity," citing this performance as one of his best. (It was released on vinyl on August 15, 1988, and nominated for a Grammy Award in 1989.)

Throughout his performance, Carlin's intense routine about cars and driving is the mirror opposite of his first routine two years earlier in *Carlin on Campus*. The former was a playful interaction with the automobile. This routine is 100 percent mock road rage, and he plays the role of the maniac. But in a brief yet powerful non sequitur, he says, "I think it's a post-Vietnam guilt syndrome of some kind. America has lost its soul, so now it's going to save its body like the fitness craze in this country. Doesn't work that way," he concludes. It's a sign of Carlin the philosopher punching above his weight, content to say something deeper about humanity.

There were more HBO specials in Carlin's future. But Jerry Hamza's daring plan was about to enter a new phase. Hamza wanted his friend to become an unforgettable icon for the ages.

He had the albums, concerts, and the television shows, but in Hamza's mind, Carlin needed something lasting and accessible. He needed to tap another medium: books.

Philosopher (1990-2008)

Twelve

Funny on Paper: Carlin in Print

For someone arguably as skilled with words as Mark Twain or Kurt Vonnegut, why did it take decades for George Carlin to issue a book? "For forty years I was using the least efficient means of communicating with people," he told Tom Snyder in 1997. "I travelled to where they live and talked to them . . . this is much better . . . send it out in a truck" (the *Late Late Show*, CBS).

Carlin's timing was good. His book was about to join a long list of humor books on the market. *SeinLanguage* by Jerry Seinfeld was a tremendous success in 1993. Paul Reiser's *Couplehood*, a *New York Times* best seller, sold more than 2 million copies following its release in 1995. Ray Romano, who starred in the very successful television sitcom *Everybody Loves Raymond*, had received an enormous advance for his first book, *Everything and a Kite*, which was published in 1998. Carlin's book deal, albeit modest by today's standards, helped him pay off his tax debt. He was uncertain whether it would sell, but it was a risk both he and his publisher were willing to take.

Brain Droppings wasn't the first book by George Carlin. In 1984, he had penned a short paperback called *Sometimes a Little Brain Damage Can Help*, which was a collection of images, illustrations, and satiric writing to be sold at his shows for $5.95. Holly Tucker designed it, and Kelly Carlin took the cover photo. It's a very colorful book inspired by *Mad* magazine in layout and presentation. Long out of print, this nine-by-twelve-inch, forty-page book often sells in the hundreds of dollars to collectors. *Brain Droppings* duplicates some of the written material first published in the concert book.

Brain Droppings focuses on three of Carlin's chosen areas of discussion: the light and whimsical, political injustices, and euphemisms in the English language. Carlin's stage appearances offer us one dimension of his work. Seeing his ideas in print makes for an uncommon experience. We get the jokes and wordplay, but we also gain insight, or what's behind the curtain of his rationale.

Laurie Abkemeier edited *Brain Droppings*. She's currently an editor and agent at the New York literary agency DeFiore & Company; back in 1996, she was a hardworking, ambitious senior editor. She recalled, "At a meeting, I believe it was Bob Miller (Founder and Vice President of Hyperion) who announced that he had just made a deal for George's book. As soon as the meeting concluded, I headed straight for my editor-in-chief's office and told him I wanted that book. That was Brian DeFiore. Brian explained that he had planned to ask Gretchen Young to take it on because he knew I already had a big list [of projects]. *No*, I said. *I want this one. I will make room for George Carlin.* I grew up on comedy and he was the gold standard." (Young edited Carlin's third book, *When Will Jesus Bring the Pork Chops?*)

The original book deal Carlin had with Hyperion was for his autobiography, but the deadline was always changing because Carlin was busy doing more than 100 shows a year. As a result, Jerry Hamza, Carlin's manager, suggested that Hyperion publish a book of his writings, including two classic pieces from his stand-up routines. Bob Miller was happy to make a deal for a second book and agreed to publish Carlin's jokes, scripts, and satire that he had collected on his computer and had never used. The autobiography would have to wait.

Abkemeier arranged all of Carlin's notes into a proper manuscript. She e-mailed, "All of the material he sent to me by mail [was] on computer disks. I think they were Mac disks, because I had to use a computer in another department on another floor to read and print out the dozens of files. Most had been saved in Impact font, which he liked and which later influenced the interior design." It was a challenging task from the start for the editor. Carlin's jokes and essays had no order to them. Afraid he would lose an idea, Carlin wrote on napkins, sticky notes, or the backs of envelopes. Then he would transpose them into subject files on his computer.

Abkemeier had a plan: "After I printed out everything, I had a mountain of random material to read through and consider. George didn't have specific thoughts on how the material should be arranged and presented, so that was my first task." At Hyperion's office in New York, she went into the boardroom to sort the pages on their enormous conference table. It took her several hours: "I spread out the entire manuscript around the perimeter of the table and went about organizing the pieces. I wanted the classic pieces to appear at equal intervals in the book. He had dozens of one-liners and very short, unrelated jokes that we came to call 'Short Takes' and divided into two parts. He had short and long essays that I wanted to arrange in a way that felt balanced. I wanted the most universal material at the start of the book, and although it's subtle, I did move loosely from theme to theme: sports, religion, sex, etc. It took many walks around the conference table, but eventually I had the material with a pacing I was happy with and in an order that also felt like a progression for the reader."

Carlin initially bristled at the cuts Abkemeier wanted to make but admitted that to her only after they talked and he agreed to the changes. In the end, Carlin enjoyed working with Abkemeier and included an acknowledgment in the published version. "We had many conversations," she recalls. "He was extraordinarily open to my edits, considering I was twenty-six, and he was hailed as a comedy genius. Even I recognized this at the time. But it wasn't difficult for me to take a firm stand with him. My job was to be his editor. I took that very seriously, and he appreciated that."

Abkemeier says she had to cut some material from the book that even she believed wasn't appropriate: "Aside from jokes that didn't quite land, there were some that were particularly violent and involved anal sex or penetration of some kind. Lord knows he was a comedian who crossed many lines, but for me, this was a line not worth crossing in the book. He heard me and agreed to cut those pieces. It wasn't a big deal."

Brain Droppings was Carlin's chance to put his ideas into print as a lasting record. His opening volley is interesting: "Don't confuse me with those who cling to hope. I enjoy describing how things are. I have no interest in how they 'ought to be.'" When the book was released, Carlin was sixty years of age. He wasn't shy about asking questions, sharing his perspective, and creating unusual lists that were to be read, not heard.

At its heart, *Brain Droppings* is a litany of complaints and grievances with sections dedicated to wordplay. Carlin's voice is clear. He rants and rambles with skill to make a point. For instance, in "Anything but the Present," Carlin expresses salient commentary regarding the media's infatuation with the past: "Our culture is composed of sequels, reruns, remakes, revivals, reissues, re-releases, recreations, re-enactments, adaptations, anniversaries, memorabilia, oldies radio and nostalgia record collections." Carlin's insightful capacity to sift through nostalgia, like most of the essays in the book, feels relevant today. Consider all the hype around the 2021 reunion of the cast of *Friends* on HBO Max. As Carlin says, "America has no now."

Carlin also takes a sharp razor to "politically correct" language. He goes to considerable length arguing that labels, names, and politically correct language is a "bogus topic" lending itself to a contextual falsehood. By labeling someone as "overweight" or with the medical term "obese" removes the more truthful term "fat" from the conversation, according to Carlin. And in a rather biting reference to a common expression these days, "people of color," the philosopher says it is "dishonest." His astute conclusion? "If you're not willing to say 'colored people,' you shouldn't be saying 'people of color.'" (In 2020, the acronym BIPOC gained currency in the English language, meaning Black, Indigenous, and people of color.)

"Politically Correct Language" is one of Carlin's strongest essays in the book. He makes jokes along the way, but he won't be fooled by American cultural labels all designed, in his opinion, to soften the impact of English and therefore truth. He hated stuff like that, sending his point home with "the pussified, trendy bullshit phrase, Native Americans," for him another abstract pretense. Then, in a bold move, he names every tribe from Adirondack to Zuni in one fulsome paragraph. "Labels divide people," Carlin writes. "We need fewer labels, not more."

Carlin's smart and satiric wordplay in the book closes with "Killer Comic," a short treatise on comedy. To him, it's a combination of a comic's desire to make people laugh while using violent language. He's referring to the proverbial style of "gallows humor," a darker, grimmer point of view echoing Kurt Vonnegut. As Carlin says, a successful night onstage for a comedian means that "they killed" or "knocked them dead" with their act. Contrast those phrases with an audience's reaction, including "I busted a gut" or "Laugh? I thought I'd die." Then Carlin sends his message: "Murder is a part of life. My society taught me that."

Carlin reveals details about his cocaine abuse in one of the few personal essays in *Brain Droppings*. In the piece called "Things Go Better," he says that the only way he could identify his heavy cocaine use was his failure to remember who won the World Series or the Super Bowl. It got so bad, he told Tom Snyder, that he tried to "wash his grass with a brush." Carlin was never afraid to joke about his "cocaine years."

Carlin worked hard to promote *Brain Droppings*. The book tour was tougher on his health than his concert tour. He often had many interviews during a typical day, either at his hotel or on a radio show or television talk show. Of the latter, Laurie Abkemeier offered her insight regarding his TV appearances: "He prepared an original piece of comedy for each show; he'd perform it and then sit in the chair and talk about the book. I told him outright that he didn't have to do this. It was a ton of work! But he insisted that if they were generous enough to have him on, he was going to give them each something special." Carlin's work ethic never let him down. He was proud of the book, and he wasn't taking anything for granted regarding its success and his reputation.

His efforts paid dividends. When the paperback edition was issued in May 1998, *Publishers Weekly* reported the book sold out its 125,000-copy first printing, and the publisher returned to press for another 20,000.

On May 11, 1997, Brenda Carlin died of cancer days after *Brain Droppings* came out in hardcover. She was fifty-seven. Her death had an enormous impact on Carlin and their daughter Kelly. In the closing moments of his July interview with Tom Snyder, he said that Brenda was "the light of my life and the keeper of my dreams."

Encouraged by the success of *Brain Droppings*, Carlin followed up with *Napalm & Silly Putty*, which Hyperion Books released in April 2001. The book spent twenty weeks on the *New York Times* bestseller list, selling about 375,000 copies over the next twelve months. Carlin was on a roll: he recorded an audiobook version that won the Grammy Award for Best Comedy Album in 2002, maintaining his place in the comedy zeitgeist. Carlin described the second book as "the same sort of drivel" as the first, but to his fans, it meant much more. Even the title has meaning: "a metaphor for Man's dual nature," combining a destructive chemical with a safe and simple toy. The book is a thoughtful mix of familiar bits from his stage act, such as "Have a nice day," combined with deeper, philosophical statements about the big picture or the macroworld, as he called it. He

Brenda and George Carlin, April 1990. ZUMA PRESS / ALAMY STOCK PHOTO

discusses homelessness, global warming, economic inequality, and airport security.

Carlin's ideas have clarity and punch in *Napalm & Silly Putty*. His thoughts, laced with anger, range widely. On the one hand, grocery shoppers who pay for breath mints with credit cards can annoy him. On the other, he can discuss bigger issues about the environment, airport security, and death with the same caustic pulse. He incorporated many of these bits into his stand-up routines for HBO, but we lose nothing as the words jolt off the page.

Two of his most affecting essays are "The Bovine Feces Trilogy" and "The Planet Is Fine, the People Are Fucked." The latter piece is a remarkable reflection on human behavior that still reverberates today. "The planet is fine. The people are fucked! It's been here over four billion years . . . and we have the nerve, the conceit to think that somehow we're a threat? . . . The planet will shake us off like a bad case of fleas . . . and it will heal itself, because that's what the planet does." This tirade marks, on paper, a statement rejecting the human species. He no longer has any interest or concern about the outcome. He's funny, profound, and unrepentant. The routine is also a memorable closer on his 1992 HBO special, *Jammin' in New York*.

"The Bovine Feces Trilogy" is Carlin's formula for detecting bullshit in the world. He offers three categories: advertising, the American political system, and religion, which he calls "the greatest bullshit story ever told!" It's rooted in his earliest days at Corpus Christi Catholic School, where he was encouraged to question his religion. Many comedians, such as Jon Stewart and Bill Maher, have picked up Carlin's ideas on these subjects and run with them. Maher released *Religulous* in 2008, a documentary that intentionally poked holes into the folly of religious doctrine from parishioners and clergy. On August 6, 2015, Jon Stewart's last program as host of Comedy Central's *Daily Show* closed with his personal message: "There is very little that you will encounter in life that has not been in some way infused with bullshit. Whenever something's been titled freedom, family, health, America take a good long sniff. It may contain traces of bullshit . . . if you smell something, say something."

To suggest that Carlin hit a nerve with *Napalm & Silly Putty* would be easy, considering his book was on the *New York Times* Best Seller list for most of 2001. This success prompted the author to add many of these ideas into his penultimate HBO special, *Life Is Worth Losing*. Carlin seems comfortable with the format, yet this book relies too much on reproducing his stand-up specials going back to 1978. Yet it has a common theme: the American political system. Carlin reveals he no longer takes part in elections, citing the meaninglessness of recycled campaign ideas, and his premise that *not* voting "gives you the right to complain," not the other way around, feeds his argument. If you vote, you get what you deserve, and you deserve what you get.

Carlin's third book of "drivel," *When Will Jesus Bring the Pork Chops?*, is his strongest statement on the human species, with a focus on society's use of language to veil reality. One-fifth of the 300-page book is devoted to euphemisms and other aspects of language that had fascinated him since childhood. For Carlin, the fear many people have of unfortunates, such as the homeless, can be found in the words and phrases that describe them. "Change its name," he writes. "It's not *home*lessness, it's *house*lessness . . . home is an abstract idea . . . these people need houses."

Carlin's writing is coherent in his last book. Like his other titles, he wrote the way he talked: clear, organized, and funny. As readers, we can't resist his position when he puts his argument this way: "You can't let the politically correct language police dictate the way you express yourself." His fight is our fight. Using the word "homeless" is a catchall for people with health issues like drug or alcohol addiction. Carlin says it intentionally keeps the definition broad and impersonal. What would he think of today's slick description of hungry people suffering *food insecurity* or the phrase for kids with chronic illness, *medically fragile children*?

The editor of the book, Gretchen Young, recalled that Carlin "was one of the most meticulous writers I have ever edited. He pored over every word and he would share his work as he went along. He'd come into the office with folders and files and notes and we would have deep focused work sessions. Every word, every passage had to flow." Young is now vice president and executive editor at Grand Central Publishing in New York. When she worked with Carlin back in 2004, the parameters of her job differed from working with a novelist: "With comedy, it is even more important to understand and to respect voice. Whereas I will completely revise a line in other forms of writing, I'm not doing that with comedy. I am clearly not messing with punch lines or the like, so it is a very different kind of editing. When it comes to comedic writing, my job is more about broad strokes like structure and flow. Does a bit belong? Maybe it doesn't speak to the book's thesis or maybe it belongs elsewhere in the manuscript."

Carlin's desire to untangle from the culture and cult of humanity seems at once selfish and liberating. His excellent poem *A Modern Man* grabs you by the scruff of the neck and makes you laugh. By the time he closes the book with "Death and Dying," a recap from his 1977 album *On the Road*, we've run the gamut of Carlin's thinking. He thought about everything, made notes, and wrote and wrote and wrote, polishing his arguments as jokes. So when the language of death, dying, and funeral services turns into a dreamy vision of one's ultimate resting place (passing away or crossing over) versus the starkness of a grave, he points out our detachment.

His most powerful statement is titled "Teams Suck!," where he takes on the notion that an individual is far better than being a team player. It was important to Carlin's own credo. He writes, "There's an *I* in independence, individuality and integrity." Often quoted on websites and coffee mugs, Carlin never said it in performance, but this was his mantra.

When the book was released, the jacket art offended an executive at the world's biggest retailer, Walmart. The cover features a mock-up of da Vinci's painting *The Last Supper*, featuring Carlin at the table holding a knife and fork. Jesus is not in the picture illustrated by Anton Markous. Walmart banned it from their stores. But you could buy it through the company's website in the privacy of your home.

The book was a success according to *Publishers Weekly*. By November 2004, Hyperion printed 375,000 copies and scheduled Carlin for a grueling book tour that took him to eighteen cities in December alone. At a hometown event, more than 700 fans turned up for a book signing at Barnes & Noble in New York's Union Square.

In the pages of *When Will Jesus Bring the Pork Chops?*, Carlin wakes us from our passive stupor about our failures as a group to communicate honestly. By distancing himself from the planet, figuratively, Carlin freed himself of any ties to the human species and the outcome of the game known as civilization. By tolerating politically correct language, he believed society was on the wrong path. His book lets us know that he's "wondering" about it all, like a true philosopher.

Gretchen Young agreed. "Carlin was in a different place when he wrote *When Will Jesus Bring the Pork Chops?* Same hilarious guy, same wonderful human, but we tend to get more philosophical as we age. His trajectory as a professional was ever upward, and *When Will Jesus Bring the Pork Chops?* is the literary culmination of George's decades-long maturation process as a comedian."

THIRTEEN

SHINY STATIONS, MOYLAN'S TAVERN, AND THE BEACON THEATRE

*A*s the last decade of the twentieth century wound its way to the next millennium, George Carlin was ready. It was twenty years since the release of his career-changing album *Class Clown*. He was gaining wider acclaim as an actor and taking more risks as a comedian. Over the next ten years, he would take another shot at a television sitcom for FOX and then, in a surprise move, take a job on a children's television show for PBS. Carlin would mark his forty years in comedy, an important milestone, but not let the grass grow under his feet.

In 1990, after three years of writing, touring, and taking care of his health after a mild heart attack, the seasoned comedian returned to New Jersey in January for an all-new special for HBO. On a stage dressed like a scene out of George Orwell's *1984*, Carlin enters with the bravado we expect. He's fifty-three, confident, and energized. It's Ronald Reagan's last year in office, and Carlin is once again pushing against authority and commenting on the language of political correctness. His self-education was paying dividends, especially in his writing. The packed venue, the 1,800-seat State Theatre in New Brunswick, was filled with an audience willing to listen and to laugh and maybe heed the words of their prophet.

Carlin starts the show with an FCC warning, and it's not what you expect. He says, "Because of the FCC, I'm never sure of what it is I'm allowed to say. So, I now have my own official policy: this is the language you will *not* be hearing tonight." He recites a long list of words and phrases, from "bottom line" to "concept when I mean idea," and Carlin commits to not saying "support group jargon from the human potential movement," such as "quality time" and "growth period," phrases that to Carlin soften the English language into a mush.

Yet this concert was as much about the macroworld as it was the microworld, the observations of an attentive comedian poised from afar. Carlin goes on about embarrassing moments because "that's the way life is; full of those little moments everybody knows them; everybody recognizes them"—life as a series of moments, like getting your underwear stuck, experiences we don't care to admit in public. To Carlin, it all matters as he takes a drink of water, proclaiming, "I don't care if it's safe or not I drink it anyway . . . because I'm an American . . . I'm not happy unless I've let government and industry poison me a little bit every day."

Carlin says there are three types of people: the "stupid," those who are "full of shit," and people who are just "fucking nuts." In Carlin's world, it doesn't take long to learn this: about eight seconds by his timing. "Think how stupid the average person is, and realize that half of them are stupider than that!" He talks about people we meet every day, quietly judging their behavior. In a direct shot, however, former Vice President Dan Quayle was all three.

Then he backs it up. "I believe you can joke about anything. It all depends on how you construct the joke . . . what the exaggeration is." He's setting us up to talk about a taboo. We do not consider rape appropriate small talk at a party, yet Carlin makes it so by making it funny and by exposing what's "permissible" in our world. So in talking about rape, he chooses animated characters as his way in. "Picture Porky Pig raping Elmer Fudd" because "Elmer had been coming on to Porky . . . he lost control." It's a funny image on a seriously unfunny topic, but Carlin takes that image to make a broader political statement: those men who have been raping the planet for centuries were doing it because Mother Earth "was asking for it!"

Doin' It Again is Carlin's most timeless performance and one of his toughest. The issues he talks about, from feminism to language control, ring as true today as they did for him in 1990. As he says, "I'm a visionary; ahead of my time. Trouble is, I'm only an hour and a half ahead." His closing routine is superb as he deconstructs a long list of racial epithets, including the volatile N-word. Says Carlin, "The context makes [words] good or bad," citing the N-word as a perfect example of identifying the racist person using the word versus the meaning of the word itself. He concludes with a pointed insight: "We don't care when Richard Pryor and Eddie Murphy say it! Why? Because we know they're not racist. They're N*****s! We don't mind their context because we know they're Black."

Carlin's most moving commentary is when he talks about words and phrases that "conceal reality." He cites the words that have been used to describe the same mental health condition of soldiers during wartime. Carlin's four-phrase list of shell shock (World War I), battle fatigue (World War II), operational exhaustion (Korean War), and post-traumatic stress disorder (Vietnam War) reflects a societal shift in using language. Today, post-traumatic stress disorder is an acceptable description of many mental health issues, even in noncombatants. "The pain is completely buried under jargon," Carlin says, "I'll bet ya, if we'd still been calling it shell shock, some of those Vietnam veterans might have got the attention they needed at the time."

Carlin's success with this, his seventh HBO special, reflects his bolder sensibility to the world and his reaction to it, a passionate dissertation about the erosion of the English language: "Smug, greedy, well-fed white people have invented a language to conceal their sins. It's as simple as that."

For Carlin, it was an important discovery. "The difference between what you see and what you know is richer and more full of possibilities," he writes in *Last Words*. "It's an accumulation of attitude and information people respond to." His next two specials for HBO would build on his newly found insights.

The show's original title for the special was *You're All Mentally Ill*. When it was released as an album, it was titled *Parental Advisory: Explicit Lyrics*.

That same year, George Carlin made an interesting and surprising choice to take the role of Mr. Conductor Jr., a character from the world of children's television. *Shining Time Station* was a new program for PBS created by Britt Allcroft and Rick Siggelkow, based on the British TV show *Thomas & Friends*, narrated by Ringo Starr, the original Mr. Conductor. Carlin's character was the cousin of Starr's and was likewise a miniaturized man who lived in the station house. He was kind, smart, and helpful at every opportunity. One of his friends is the character Billy Twofeathers, played by Canadian actor Tom Jackson. Twofeathers fixed the engines in the station to keep them in top shape; we often saw the pair in the station's workshop, with Carlin on the worktable. (Mr. Conductor was only eighteen inches tall.) Didi Conn, who played Frenchie in the movie version of the musical *Grease*, was Stacy Jones, the stationmaster. The show incorporated animated elements from the British show with fresh stories told by Mr. Conductor.

PBS was proud to have Carlin on board. The producer and creator of the series, Britt Allcroft, met with him after hearing his piece "A Place for My Stuff," which impressed her. As she recalled in an essay for the *Los Angeles Times*, "Although the words were aimed at adults, I heard a universal voice. I heard a sound that, for children, could be intimate, lyrical, sometimes spooky, soothing and, most important, kind" (June 26, 2008). Carlin played the role of Mr. Conductor for forty-five episodes from 1991 to 1993, almost always in front of a green screen, looped into the main frame of the show. The role had some appeal because Mr. Conductor was unpretentious and well written. Allcroft agreed that Carlin was right for the part, but she also felt that he might have been filling a void in his life. Like her, Carlin had some lonely years as a child. She said the show "was one way we expressed it creatively."

It wasn't a smooth transition for Carlin the performer. Despite his optimism going into the project, Allcroft reports that Carlin's initial hesitancy was in the sound booth used to record his voice-overs for the *Thomas the Tank Engine* segments. In his first session in Toronto, Carlin still needed an audience to get through it. He was provided with one: a teddy bear. After the series ended, Carlin and his wife Brenda gave Allcroft a teddy bear named Teddy Carlin as a parting gift. It was their way of saying thank you. Allcroft, now retired, found a place for it on her piano.

Carlin expresses deep gratitude for participating in the show in his memoir. He says he enjoyed doing it because he wanted to surprise his adult audience with his versatility. Even at this stage in his extraordinary career, Carlin was still trying to prove something.

"I don't believe anything the government tells me," declares George Carlin in front of a sold-out Paramount Theater, launching his favorite HBO special, *Jammin' in New York*, originally broadcast live on April 25, 1992. It was about a year after Carlin suffered his third heart attack in Las Vegas, yet he seems remarkably strong, full of energy, and ready to "leave the symbols [flags and so on] to the symbol minded." He spends the first ten minutes of the show commenting on the Gulf War based on his premise that G-men who need to prove that they have the "bigger dicks" in the world leads to warfare. His routine "Rockets and Penises in the Persian Gulf" is delivered with zeal. He was tapping into his rage for this hunk. It was a choice he made a few years earlier when he needed to stay current and rebuff the success of Sam Kinison, whose shrieking rage was pushing the art of comedy into new avenues. In fact, Kinison died two weeks before the broadcast. Carlin dedicated the show to him.

Carlin always found a balance in his shows between rhetoric and lighter quick takes. For instance, to contrast his opening bit about the war, Carlin works in a piece called "Little Things We Share," such as cringing after drinking grapefruit juice or trying to urinate during a sneeze. He pokes fun at "Airline Announcements" and the weird combinations they often contain, such as "pre-boarding," "nonstop flights," "near miss versus near hit," or "put your seat back, forward," and his favorite part of a flight, the safety procedures. "All destinations are final," says Carlin, closing with the "unfortunate word, terminal."

He continues with a rant against the "arrogant elitist" game of golf. In one swing of mathematical geographic calculation, Carlin says that homelessness can be solved. Build on the "3 million acres or 4,820 square miles" that make up the American golf scene. And why stop there? Cemeteries, like golf courses, should recycle dead bodies into the ecology of the environment. The system is "beginning to collapse and everything is starting to break down" is the point. He relishes the word "entropy," used to describe thermodynamic degeneration. For Carlin, it's the slow collapse of civilization that he enjoys, professing that he "loves bad news" because to him it's entertaining.

This all leads to his final, profound routine, "The Planet Is Fine." Carlin's powerful closing argument, if you will, reflects a man who's done some serious thinking about the human species. He breaks it down to one word, arrogance. Controlling nature by humans, he argues, got us into the mess we're in now. Even some thirty years after this performance, his remarks carry significant weight as hurricanes rage, wildfires burn, and people die of extreme heat in 2021. "We haven't learned how to help each other. How can we help the planet?" he asks. His conclusion? "The planet is fine; the people are fucked." His frightening prediction of a mutating virus to kick people off the planet like fleas cuts deep during COVID-19, with more than 6 million people dead. But he leaves us with a morsel of hope. "I think we're a part of a greater wisdom that we'll never understand. A higher order . . . I call it the big electron . . . it doesn't punish, it doesn't reward, it doesn't judge; it just is and so are we." They released the bulk of this excellent performance on a CD, with the same title, winning Carlin another Grammy Award in 1993.

In 1994, Carlin finally caved to one of the many requests for him to produce and star in a sitcom. He'd been putting it off since *Apt 2C* failed to get the proverbial green light. FOX made him a better offer. One of the network's edgiest sitcoms was *Married... with Children*, starring Ed O'Neill and Katey Sagal. Fans would tune in Sunday nights at 9 p.m., sending the ratings and the show into cult status. When Carlin agreed to produce a weekly sitcom, FOX gave him the 9:30 p.m. time slot following *Married... with Children*. It was the perfect lead-in, said Carlin in interviews.

In her memoir, Kelly Carlin said that her father was tired of touring and ready to settle into a different mode of work. After nearly three decades logging thousands of miles on the road, doing concerts, talk shows, and HBO specials, Carlin, the elder, was ready to settle down. His home life was suffering: Kelly was getting over an awful marriage and her own drug addiction, and Brenda was in recovery for alcoholism but struggling with other health issues. Carlin wanted to spend more time at home rather than fly out every three days to perform. Working on a sitcom in Los Angeles, close to home with regular hours, seemed like a good idea. So in the fall of 1993, Carlin went to work.

The show was cocreated by Carlin with Sam Michael Simon, the Stanford University graduate whose claim to fame was *The Simpsons*. He was a producer, writer, and director and once managed a professional boxer. Born in 1955, Simon grew up in Beverly Hills. His neighbor was Groucho Marx. He drew cartoons for the *Stanford Daily*, the student-run university newspaper. Simon majored in psychology but never pursued it with any fervor because he got work as a cartoonist, first with the *San Francisco Chronicle*, then at Filmation Studios, the animation production company.

While at Filmation, Simon developed his writing skills. (He was a natural at comedy.) They encouraged him to take a stab at television, so he submitted a script for the ABC sitcom *Taxi*, starring Judd Hirsch and Danny DeVito. It was so good that the show produced it and hired Simon as a writer. He was twenty-eight years of age. Like George Carlin, who teamed up with Jack Burns and took a chance on Hollywood in 1960, Sam Simon joined producer James L. Brooks and animator Matt Groening to develop *The Simpsons*, the animated adult comedy that's been a weekly staple at FOX since 1989.

Simon was a creative supervisor on *The Simpsons*. He assembled the very first writing team to transform animated shorts on the *Tracey Ullman Show* into thirteen half-hour episodes. Some called him the "unsung hero" of the series, disliked by some staff members who knew him as a control freak and difficult to work with. In 1990, Simon put it another way when he told Joe Morgenstern of the *Los Angeles Times*, "I've never worked on a good show where there isn't a certain amount of creative friction. I've seen brother turn against brother in a rewrite room." That didn't change when he started working with George Carlin.

The FOX show centered on the life of the character George O'Grady, a New York taxi driver, played by Carlin. (It was his grandmother's maiden name.) The principal action took place in a tavern called Moylan's, named after Carlin's own watering hole in Morningside Heights. The bartender/owner was Jack Donahue, named after the actual owner of the Moylan, Jimmy Donahue. Anthony Starke played him. Actor Alex Rocco played George's best friend, Harry Rossetti. Rocco was a veteran theater actor whose most famous role was that of Moe Greene, the Vegas nightclub owner in *The Godfather* who suffers the ire of Michael Corleone (Al Pacino) while lying on a massage table. Paige French played server Sydney Paris, and Mike Hagerty played Moylan's regular patron, Frank MacNamara. Susan Sullivan played George's love interest, Kathleen Rachowski, a pet-store operator. Of the twenty-seven episodes produced, Sullivan appears in only seven, which is a pity because she and Carlin have good chemistry on those episodes.

Carlin was a part of a group of creative people, one of the few where he felt he belonged. The experience was the same as *Outrageous Fortune* and *Working Tra$h*, two of Carlin's most successful and satisfying acting jobs. His wife Brenda was also happy that her husband was coming home after work instead of catching a flight to another city without her. Daughter Kelly agreed in her memoir *A Carlin Home Companion*. She saw this opportunity as a chance that her father might slow down his work effort and "retire to Big Sur" after his third heart attack. Besides, she believed he earned a show of his own just like *Seinfeld*, *Roseanne*, *Mad About You* with Paul Reiser, and *Home Improvement* with Tim Allen, which were getting big ratings in the television sitcom wars. In Kelly's mind, it was time for her father, a seasoned actor, writer, and comedian, to join the fray.

Carlin was happy to be on the Warner Bros. Studio lot, especially Stage 17, where they produced the show. He was on sacred ground: Humphrey Bogart, James Cagney, and Joan Crawford shot some of their best work there, including *Casablanca*, *Yankee Doodle Dandy*, and *Mildred Pierce*, respectively. His family was welcome too; Kelly, Brenda, and his brother Patrick were regulars on the set.

The George Carlin Show debuted on January 16, 1994, with an episode titled "When Unexpected Things Happen to George." It was cowritten by Carlin and Sam Simon, one of only two episodes in which the featured star has a writing credit. Simon led the writing team and supervised all twenty-nine episodes that were produced. That team included Carlin's brother Patrick, who penned "George

Plays a Mean Pinball" in season 1, and daughter Kelly and her husband Bob McCall, who wrote "George Pulls the Plug" in season 2.

The show has a few merits. First, it was conscious of George Carlin's celebrity as a comedian. George O'Grady has plenty of punch lines, which could have been written by the stand-up comic. (He had retained the ability to edit and revise his dialogue.) Second, they built the story lines around Carlin's life. In the episode called "George Goes on a Date, Part 2," Kathleen Rachowski (Susan Sullivan) asks him during a dinner scene in an Italian restaurant why he hasn't seen a movie for such a long time. George replies, "I usually wait until they're on network TV, then I know it's gonna be good." Kathleen replies that she still prefers to *go* to the movies, to which George replies, "I would go with you! Is there anything new coming out with Danny Kaye in it?," getting a merry laugh. Little does the audience know that Kaye, who died in 1987, was one of Carlin's silver screen idols.

Just a few days before the sitcom's debut, Carlin appeared on the *Late Show* with David Letterman. He performed a stock favorite routine, "Baseball and Football," a piece he rarely performed after 1990. Once he sat down, Letterman reminded him he was on the original stage for the *Ed Sullivan Show*, of which Carlin said he was experiencing a sense of fear. The host put Carlin at ease. He talked about getting his first sitcom, fully embracing its promise. He describes O'Grady as a guy from the Upper West Side of New York who never left the neighborhood. More telling is Carlin's hopes for the show: "I've never been happier in a creative setting all the time I've done stand-up or a couple of movies or a guest shot here and there. We're doing good work . . . and I hope we can catch an audience. It's feeling very true and very right."

Considering that network executives considered this show a "smart sitcom," FOX was always wary of Carlin's history with the FCC. In fact, they read every script in advance before going into production. One example is an episode called "George Speaks His

Mind." The original title was "George Says Fuck," but in a memo dated April 9, 1994, the network's policy editor, attorney Linda Shima-Tsuno, asked Sam Simon to cut the F-bomb from the title and from the script. Shima-Tsuno's polite, specific, and assertive memo shows FOX wasn't about to gamble on any ruling (or potential ruling) by the FCC that would endanger their broadcasting license. Her job in the standards and practices department at FOX was to review material for acceptability for broadcast. In a piece for the March 1997 issue of *Harper's*, she called herself "a sheriff for toon town." That said, the "George Speaks His Mind" feature is notable for leaving *in* the F-words, though they are bleeped.

In a nod to Carlin's political humor, a dream sequence on the same episode gives the star a chance to take a shot at the founding fathers, who visit him one night. "Freedom of speech isn't for all Americans," O'Grady exclaims. "Just for guys like you: rich, white, male slaveholding landowners who, in framing the Constitution . . . conspicuously denied voting rights to women, slaves, Indians and people who didn't own property." Then Washington, Franklin, and Jefferson give each other a high-five.

For George Carlin, an artist who believed the First Amendment protected his right to free speech, it must have been annoying to know that the network he was working for vetted every word. Either that or "George Says Fuck" was an attempt to push back. Regardless, it wasn't the reason FOX canceled the series after its second season. Someone did not fully commit the network to producing a "smart white show" after a "dumb white show" like *Married... with Children*. In his memoir, Carlin says that the network wasn't interested in promoting the show because the publicists hated it—this and the fact that Sam Simon was "a fucking horrible person to be around" (*Last Words*).

Much like his years in the U.S. Air Force, Carlin always ran into authority that he believed stifled his freedom. It was the same at

FOX. To him, the "corporate crap" of working on a scheduled network television show was too much because he felt like a Hollywood outsider, not a player. He loved acting but hated showbiz culture. The *George Carlin Show* was a valiant effort, but after working seventy-hour weeks, having his scripts vetted for potentially offensive material, and working with a horrible show runner, Carlin got his secret wish, and FOX canceled the series after two exhausting years. He went back to the network that loved him, HBO.

New York's Beacon Theatre was the site of Carlin's next three HBO specials. It was home. Built in 1929, the Beacon is most notable for some legendary concerts by the Allman Brothers, who entertained audiences more than 200 times from 1989 to 2014. In 1996, they booked Carlin to do a live broadcast for HBO on the stage of the Upper West Side venue, a show he named "Back in Town." This was Carlin's most challenging presentation yet. With the failed sitcom

Principal cast of the short-lived Fox TV show: from the left Alex Rocco, Christopher Rich, Paige French, George Carlin, Anthony Starke, Susan Sullivan.
FOX/PHOTOFEST

behind him, Carlin was free to go back to his comfortable perch and talk about the bigger issues of the day, such as abortion, capital punishment, and the American prison system.

The audience leaps to its collective feet when Carlin enters from right outside the stage door. Wasting no time, he asks, "Why, why, why, why is it that most of the people who are against abortion are people you wouldn't want to fuck in the first place?," launching without a flinch a rhetorical question. It's also the opening question on his album *A Place for My Stuff*, issued in 1981. Only this time, it's part of his first routine, "Sanctity of Life," a well-considered piece, critical of the conservative pro-life movement. Carlin finds the loopholes in their argument: "If you're preborn you're fine. If you're preschool, you're fucked!," adding that "conservatives want live babies so that they can raise them to be dead soldiers." This routine circulated widely on social media when *Roe v. Wade* made the news in 2022. All this leads to a twenty-minute hunk regarding capital punishment, which Carlin thinks should include crucifixions, boiling people in oil, and "Preparation H-Bomb," using nuclear weapons to kill criminals. Carlin's anger-fueled monologue gets huge laughs and steady applause of approval in front of what he calls my "Judeo-Christian friends."

Carlin goes further. His eight-minute satire of "State Prison Farms" is a dark series of ideas that takes four groups of people—criminals, sex offenders, addicts, and "maniacs and crazy people"—by assigning a state where they can all coexist, an American internment camp if you like. Carlin suggests that Kansas, Wyoming, Utah, and Colorado are appropriate. His plan is absurd yet rooted in a kernel of truth for some conservative, right-wing thinkers who, in his opinion, would rather lock people up and throw away the key.

In contrast, Carlin explores more fart jokes, then goes into his reliable creation, a list of twenty-four things that piss him off. He calls it "Free-Floating Hostility," which includes people who use physical quotation marks in their conversations and advising those people "whose needs are not being met to drop some of your needs." But his most profound statement comes when he questions the need for people to document everything they do on camcorders, the 1990s version of a smartphone. The sage asks, "Does experience have to be saved and put on a shelf?" He closes with his last insightful complaint: American politicians born and raised in a familiar system he defines as "Garbage in. Garbage out."

On this special, his ninth for HBO, Carlin has refined his thinking. In his memoir, he cites this show as an important marker in his life and art: "The longer you live, the richer your matrix gets . . . the difference between what you see and what you know is richer and more full of possibilities . . . after a certain age you get points for not being dead" (*Last Words*). *Back in Town* shows a vibrant Carlin, alert to the changing culture in America. His next HBO special, which marked forty years in comedy, gave him time to pause, reflect, and consider his next step.

The special, recorded in 1997 in part at the Wheeler Opera House in Aspen, Colorado, is a hybrid. The first quarter of the show features Carlin's best routines of the past forty years, starting in 1963 on a show called *Talent Scouts*. It's quite the highlight reel. In chronological order, we hear and see Carlin's transformation from the young clean-cut jester to the older, graying philosopher. But the sixty-year-old will not take his past work for granted.

Before sitting down with host Jon Stewart, Carlin does thirty minutes of new material, beginning with a poem he calls "Advertising" aka "Advertising Lullaby," which would be reproduced in *Napalm & Silly Putty*. The work reflects an active, imaginative artist whose love of words never fails him. For this work, he connects the dots between advertising, religion, and the thread between all of them, "bullshit." "Quality, value, style, service, selection, convenience . . . come on in for a free demonstration and a free consultation with our friendly, professional staff. . . . Actually, it's our way of saying, 'Bend over just a little further, so we can stick this big advertising dick up your ass.'"

Most of this routine was being road tested for Carlin's next HBO special, *You Are All Diseased*, but his presentation here is so polished that there's little difference in both versions. He took nothing to the stage without working the material into presentable shape. As a change of pace, Carlin invites us into his microworld with a bit about his dogs Tippy, Annie, Murphy, and Moe and his cat Vern.

The best part of the one-hour special is the last quarter when Stewart interviews Carlin about his life, including his use of drugs (and why they no longer work for him). But most important was his reply to Stewart's question, "Why not retire?," to which Carlin, in a spirited and thoughtful response, says, "An artist has an obligation to be en route. To be going somewhere; there's a journey involved. You don't know where it is, but that's the fun. So, you're always going to be seeking and going and challenging yourself . . . it drives you; trying to be fresh, calling on yourself."

Stewart's last question, "Do you feel your place in comedy?," gets another funny remark from Carlin: "Longevity is a wonderful thing. Sometimes you get applause just for not being dead." Yet when he talks about his love of individuals, a more philosophical Carlin emerges: "You can see the universe in their eyes so cumulatively I've gotten so that I feel that I'm part of a big extended family. A family I never really had, by the way."

Carlin ends the interview by complimenting Stewart: "You're gonna show us a lot and I look forward to it." They nominated the HBO program for two Primetime Emmy Awards and three CableACE Awards, winning for Best Stand-Up Comedy Special and Best Writing an Entertainment Special. Two years later, Stewart became the host of the *Daily Show* on Comedy Central. Not one to rest on his laurels, Carlin went back to work.

On February 6, 1999, three years after his last HBO special, George Carlin took charge of the Beacon Theatre stage like a man possessed. *You Are All Diseased* was an important show. Two years earlier, his wife Brenda had died, and he had released *Brain Droppings* to wide acclaim. As a way of making sense of his grief and new successes, he looked to the cosmos and took up astronomy. He was searching for answers beyond the stars and looking to nest in the Oort cloud for a better view. This special was an opportunity for him to try.

Carlin was always confident in his material before taking it to the HBO stage. But on January 9, 1999, he made an exception and performed two shows at the legendary Comedy Store in Los Angeles. Footage of his act, recorded for his own archive, was released after his death on *The Best of George Carlin* DVD collection in 2019. It's quite the show. Opening with a breathless thirteen-minute rant, Carlin riffs on airport security, germ phobia, and American fears over terrorist groups. He's getting laughs and occasional applause from an audience sipping their cocktails. They're happy to see him yet overwhelmed by Carlin's caustic presentation. In a small club, in this case the main room, the emotional intent of his act seems too much to bear. About 400 patrons jammed the Comedy Store; the Beacon has a capacity of 2,800. But Carlin delivers his material the same way in both settings, perhaps with a little less projection in the Comedy Store since the people up front were literally in reach.

Carlin exclaims, "What is all this shit about angels? Three out of four people now believe in angels. What are you fucking stupid? I think it's a massive, collective, psychotic chemical flashback from all the drugs smoked, swallowed, snorted, shot and absorbed rectally by all Americans from 1960 to 1990. Thirty years of adulterated street drugs will get you some fucking angels, my friend." Carlin loved to share his ideas with an audience. He put it best to Jay Dixit at *Psychology Today*: "It's like conducting an orchestra . . . and you're just waving the baton and bringing them in, leading them forward and it's just a nice kind of feeling" (June 23, 2008).

That feeling carried over to the Beacon Theatre performance of February 9, 1999. Carlin's perch is a rooftop set for this show. He opens with a "Fuck you!," as he says, because he's "just trying to make you feel at home." The comedian admits to having no pet peeves but "major, psychotic hatreds," his way of opening with a series of complaints, rooted in powerful observations. It's the same set from the Comedy Store. "Airport Security," written and performed two years before security got tight after 9/11, reflects Carlin's remarkable powers of observation. To him, airport security "makes white people feel safe" while "reducing your liberty and reminding you that they can fuck with you anytime they want." Carlin recycles history for his own purpose. In 1768, Benjamin Franklin wrote that "those who would give up essential liberty to purchase a little temporary safety deserve neither liberty nor safety." But Carlin has a better closer: "That's the way Americans are now. They're always willing to trade away a little of their freedom in exchange for the feeling, the *illusion*, of security."

Carlin gave himself license to write a new piece about kids who are glorified by parents in society. He worked on "Kids and Parents" for years until he unleashed it with gusto on *You Are All Diseased*. This hunk reflected Mr. Conductor's darker side, and Carlin wasn't afraid to mention that fact in the bit, either. "Your children are overrated . . . they're not all cute . . . not all children are smart and clever . . . kids are like any other group of people: a few winners, a whole lot of losers!" Carlin's hilarious rants like this make people uncomfortable but only long enough for him to plant a thought. "I think what every child needs and ought to have every day is two hours of daydreaming."

Carlin's ability to sustain the furious energy he taps into for an hour is remarkable. It's almost performance art, and in his memoir, Carlin writes that he had given himself permission to be a "clinical sociopath." He was responding to the angry comics, such as Sam

Kinison and Lewis Black, for example. Going "angry" in stand-up comedy might be authentic, but it's risky. A comedian could be equally repelling as engaging. For Carlin, the anger was merely theatrical. It was a means to an end, an exaggeration yet based on his disappointment in the choices humans make.

Jerry Seinfeld said it best in David Steinberg's book *Inside Comedy* (2021). He describes the importance of a stand-up's environment: "There's nothing better for a comedian than being hemmed in, having been closed off, shut out, not welcome; that's nutrition." That nutrition distinguishes this special from all the rest. Carlin is angry because he feels trapped by the stupidity and absurdity of the system, one he could no longer trust.

When Brenda Carlin died in 1997, George and daughter Kelly went into mourning. During those dark months, they retreated to a cabin in Yosemite Valley for three days. To Kelly, who had spent many birthdays and holidays without her working father, it was "like a hundred Christmases times a thousand birthdays" (*A Carlin Home Companion*). They spread Brenda's ashes in two places: into the Merced River and near a giant redwood tree in Mariposa Grove. While George found closure after the valley stay, Kelly continued to carve her own path for the next two years while coming to grips with her mother's death. In 1999, she was accepted into the prestigious Pacifica Graduate Institute near Santa Barbara, California, to study the ideas of Carl Jung and Joseph Campbell. It led to a master's degree in counseling psychology.

In her memoir, Kelly talks about the time she learned that her dad "met someone" in 1998. Her name was Sally Wade, and she met George in an independent bookstore called Dutton's in Los Angeles. For Kelly, it was upsetting news. She felt uncomfortable because the two of them had been bonding as father and daughter in their grief. For her dad, who was trying to move on, it was love at first sight. But he waited a few months before asking Wade for a date.

Wade lived in Venice Beach, California, across the street from writer and performer Orson Bean. By the time Carlin met her, she was an established writer and producer in Hollywood. Her résumé included work on the 1970s hit show *What's Happening*. In her light yet thoughtful book *The George Carlin Letters* (2011), she offers some insight into their relationship, Carlin's work ethic, and their love life. While it doesn't have the emotional weight of Kelly Carlin's memoir, it has some interesting revelations about Carlin the man.

Wade and Carlin loved each other deeply. They often joked about their cosmic origins from Jupiter because there was no way that two people like them could've surfaced from Earth. Perhaps it was Carlin's interest in astronomy that carried the pair forward spiritually. Wade met Carlin when he was transitioning his point of view to the edges of the universe, the Oort cloud. Jupiter was closer to home than Earth in his mind. So the pair embraced the concept of being from Jupiter, "which is where we believe we're from and where we'll end up someday" (*The George Carlin Letters*).

Wade never married Carlin, even though he asked her on a weekly basis. (One of Carlin's marriage proposal notes is reproduced in her book.) They deeply entwined their lives, according to Wade, as a working, affectionate couple that thoroughly enjoyed each other's company. He called her his "spouse without papers" because he hated the phrase "significant other." Wade shares dozens of handwritten notes, postcards, and photographs the pair exchanged over their ten-year relationship. While HBO gave him a creative lifeline, Sally Wade provided him with the grounded support and love that he needed to continue to work, and the feeling was mutual. She writes, "Our love was instant. George had a huge, huge heart," adding that "it was love and stars and Jupiter and the moon, and bridges, and I just soaked it in."

It's important to note that Carlin's tough veneer in performance, especially during his HBO specials after 1998, was his stage persona.

Offstage, he was quiet, calm, and not looking for approval. Wade's book points out his sensitivity as a human being and depicts Carlin as in his element as a youthful, sixty-two-year-old in Wade's company. He called her every night after a gig and sent her postcards from Las Vegas. She writes, "As soon as George walked offstage, he became who he really was: the finest person I've ever known."

In 2016, the estate of George Carlin released an important album called *I Kinda Like It When a Lotta People Die* on the label Eardrum. (The title phrase was from Carlin's brother Patrick.) Six of the tracks were from a cassette recording made during Carlin's residency at the MGM Grand in Las Vegas on September 9 and 10, 2001. The new material was originally planned for use in Carlin's upcoming HBO special, his twelfth, scheduled for November—barely two months after the destructive events of September 11, 2001.

Carlin enjoyed his ongoing HBO gig because it gave him the financial and creative incentive to work hard and write new material every couple of years. The booking at the Beacon Theatre was no different in scope from the previous commitments. Yet for reasons that went against his better judgment, the show's title was changed to *Complaints & Grievances*. For a guy who was fearless in his work, the change comes as a bit of a compromise, one that he made to placate the public and HBO. James Sullivan reports that Carlin changed the title, saying the record company, Atlantic, "had no balls" for the album title and its release after 9/11.

For some comedians, the shocking event that is now referred to as 9/11 changed the rules of the game. Was irony dead, as some comedians asked? David Letterman said he "couldn't trust his judgment" anymore, and Jon Stewart, the steadfast critic of American politics on the *Daily Show*, pulled back by choosing what writer Sascha Cohen would later describe as "reflexive patriotism" in a 2021 essay in *The Atlantic*. Cohen writes that at the time, "September 11 was quickly made into something hallowed and untouchable."

On a Comedy Central special in November 2001, Gilbert Gottfried, the acerbic New York comedian, told a joke that he wanted to take a direct flight to California but couldn't because "the plane had to stop at the Empire State Building first." The Los Angeles audience jeered him. Maybe there are some events that are "untouchable" but not for the comedian from Morningside Heights. Gottfried died in 2022. Like his joke about 9/11, his death was too soon.

Carlin was in the best position, the Oort cloud, to make a joke about 9/11. His routine "I Kinda Like It When a Lotta People Die" had not originally been a topical piece, but because of the events of 9/11, it had assumed a new context, like his earlier hunk on airport security. He could control the words but not the situation.

In the summer prior to his 2001 special, the MGM Grand in Las Vegas had been home to Carlin's annual tenure for several weeks. He wrote during the day and performed at night, often sequestered in a nearby condo. Jerry Hamza, his friend and manager, says that Carlin usually rose early in the morning to write many ideas that occurred to him that day or the night before. Hamza says, on a bonus track from the 2016 release, that he heard the "I Kinda Like It When A Lotta People Die" routine more than sixty times during the Vegas run. He says it was going to close the HBO special in November, and despite its emotional intensity, Carlin knew his audience "would accept that from him."

Carlin would open his Vegas show with the political satire "Rats and Squealers" with a proclamation that "we're living in a nation of stool pigeons . . . an open invitation to be a rat." Carlin had a twisted admiration for people who have a code regardless if they are breaking the law. Then he takes us to the next satiric level. "I love the crooks. I don't care if they come to my house and kill my entire family!" He says he used to cheer them on in movies, happy to see a crook break out from the system and act as an individual, the gist of Carlin's opening rant.

At one point, he even mentions Osama Bin Laden—then known primarily for his involvement in terrorist bombings outside the United States—as a punch line to a joke about aircraft explosions. But when he reaches a piece called "Uncle Dave," we hear the thrust of his routine: "I'm into fatal disasters; I kinda like it when lotta people die . . . you can never have too many dead people . . . because I really like big disasters . . . tornadoes, hurricanes, earthquakes, aftershocks, tidal waves, famine, forest fires or, even better, a flaming asteroid." It's a setup for a longer diatribe, a breathless description of an extreme scenario where everything turns into "liquid hate. A big pool of liquid hate; and the hate pool spins faster and faster; and it begins to expand at a rapid rate; bigger and bigger until the pool of hate is bigger than the universe until suddenly it explodes into a million tiny stars . . . until Uncle Dave wins the lottery every week and Uncle Dave is finally happy. And that is why I like it when a lotta people die."

Carlin worked on the piece for months, shaping and perfecting it. He considered it an extension of "The Planet Is Fine" routine but in the extreme. In his memoir, he discusses its creation as a kind of characterization of the "clinical sociopath" encouraged by people's laughter, tapping into the near-universal thrill of watching a natural disaster unfold on television. "I can't help it, it just makes me feel good." As he reveals in a June 23, 2001, club performance, "I'm here for the fun . . . to me the world is one big fucking show . . . and I say there's no second show . . . so enjoy it while you can."

As a satiric, irreverent work of art, "I Kinda Like It When a Whole Lotta People Die" stands the test of time. Yet the finished piece, which Carlin had worked on starting back in 1999, wasn't appropriate by September 12, 2001. Carlin admits to being a "realist" about this in his memoir: "Osama bin fucking Laden hadn't just blown up the World Trade Center. He'd blown up the best piece I'd written in ten years" (*Last Words*).

Six weeks after the events of 9/11, it was on with the show. It surprised director Rocco Urbisci that HBO did not cancel, but he and Carlin forged ahead. In a short interview track on the 2016 album, Urbisci, who directed Carlin's last ten specials for HBO, said the timing of the show was important to George: "He was from New York. This was his hometown. They fucked on his turf!" He adds, "The audience was great; they were looking for some relief. I think they were grateful that he came."

Complaints & Grievances debuted live on November 17, 2001. The Beacon Theatre stage was made to look like a construction site in a neighborhood not unlike Carlin's own. Before he says a word, the packed house rises when he arrives onstage. Their love is palpable. To address the elephant in the room, Carlin reminds us about his New York credentials: born in New York Hospital, grew up in Morningside Heights, and so on. By acknowledging the events of 9/11, "the turd in the punch bowl" Carlin puts his blue-collar roots firmly in line with the audience. He feels angry that someone messed with his home turf, and the kid who learned how to stand up for his rights on West 49th Street was ready for a fight. His plan? A FART squad to smoke out the enemy in the caves and hideaways in Afghanistan with a domestic team led by Rudy Giuliani, "an Italian from Brooklyn" who could get the job done. He doesn't specify what that job is, but it doesn't matter. It was just what this audience wanted, even needed, to hear: let's kick some ass!

"Now let's do to the show I was planning on right up until September 10," declares Carlin, ready to complain about driving, self-help advice, and singers with one name. Missing from the set is "I Kinda Like It When a Lotta People Die." This show is about connecting with people through Carlin's microworld, talking about parts of the body and the stuff we all notice and/or do, such as finding a scab on your head or clipping your toenails and playing with them because "it just came off your body, there's still moisture in it. It's almost alive!"

Carlin's delivery features fast, bebop-style explosions of words, with the performer pausing only occasionally to catch his breath. He was never short of subjects to complain about. He gave up on taboos years ago, opening himself up to explore even the most sacred of subjects à la Lenny Bruce. In this respect, his piece called "A List of People Who Oughta Be Killed" is a good example. Starting with people who read self-help books, Carlin uses his reliable rhetorical style: "If you're looking for self-help, why would you read a book by somebody else?" His list continues with motivational speakers, Yuppie parents, southern rednecks, people who wear visors, and white guys who shave their heads completely bald. Carlin's routine is deflecting the pain and shock of 9/11 by using a sledgehammer of commentary to criticize other people.

He closes the show with his brilliant routine on the Ten Commandments and why they should be reduced to two. (It would later be included in *When Will Jesus Bring the Pork Chops?*) The first three commandments can be "thrown out" because they contain "spooky language" designed to "scare and control primitive people," says Carlin. By reducing the ten to two, Carlin's logic puts him at the top of the class. "Murder. The Fifth Commandment . . . you realize that religion has never really had a problem with murder . . . it just depends on who's doing the killing and who's getting killed." For this show at this critical time in history, hearing from George Carlin was, in the words of Lewis Black, like "a call from an old friend that you think of and when you do, it always makes you smile" (liner notes to *I Kinda Like It When a Lotta People Die*).

In 1952, Bishop Fulton J. Sheen debuted on television with a program about faith called *Life Is Worth Living*. It ran for three years on the now-defunct DuMont network. The half-hour program featured the Catholic bishop talking about moral issues. He often started with a funny story to draw you in: humor as an effective way to get your attention and ingratiate yourself. It's uncertain if George Carlin was one of the millions of viewers Sheen pulled in every Sunday in those early days of television, but he certainly had the bishop in mind when he called his 2005 special for HBO *Life Is Worth Losing*. But instead of the Sheen blackboard, which the cloaked bishop used to teach the Gospel, Carlin's stage features a snow-covered cemetery with a full moon looming large in the backdrop. It wasn't just another George Carlin show.

After the astonishing opening bit called "A Modern Man," Carlin admits to being "341 days sober." It was a rare and important disclosure because in December 2004, he had checked himself into a rehab clinic. He woke up one day, encouraged by his new belle, Sally Wade, to kick the opiate Vicodin as well as his beloved red wine, which he often used to wash down six tabs a day. Although he stopped performing for thirty days while detoxing at Promises, the clinic in Malibu, he didn't drop any other performances during 2005. Carlin talks about his recovery in *Last Words*, stating that the doctrine of Alcoholics Anonymous was as successful for him as it was for his late wife Brenda during her recovery in the 1990s. He says that it "worked" and that he wasn't just kicking Vicodin and wine but also ending some five decades of drug and alcohol abuse that started when he smoked his first joint at age thirteen.

The results are striking: Carlin's energy is much calmer on this show. He looks older yet comfortable in his own skin despite his stiff movements. Now, the better part of a year out of rehab, he felt strong enough to carry on at a slower, less caustic pace.

Carlin's analysis called "Extreme Human Behavior" starts with a rant about suicide, followed by his funny thoughts on murder, genocide, human sacrifice, and necrophilia. It's gallows humor at its finest. He talks about what would happen if the world no longer had electricity. In Carlin's doomsday scenario, we would return to the barbaric days of Cro-Magnon man to survive while prisons and nuthouses would unleash millions of armed robbers, rapists, murderers, carjackers, kidnappers, pushers, junkies, gang members, and mobsters: "our old friends at camp." Carlin's intention is to soften the audience up for his "All-Suicide Channel." Taking a hint from his classic "The Planet Is Fine, the People Are Fucked" routine, Carlin reaches a new conclusion: "Only a nation of unenlightened half-wits could have taken this beautiful place and turn it into what it is today: a shopping mall . . . a big fucking shopping mall."

Carlin closes the seventy-five-minute performance with "Coast-to-Coast Emergency," a revised version of "I Kinda Like It When a Lotta People Die." He took little out of the original version from 2001 because he knew the piece was solid: a work so intense in emotion and so well written that it would make the Book of Revelations seem like a story for children.

His closing line changes from "Now you know why I like it when a lotta people die" to "Now do you see why I like it when Nature gets even with humans?" By taking himself out of the equation, he becomes a sage. To change the "Uncle Dave" or "I Kinda Like It When a Lotta People Die" piece from the personal to the philosophical gives it more weight. He not only makes us laugh but also engages our imagination. The album recording of the special was released in January 2006 on Eardrum records with the same title. It was nominated for a Grammy Award, Carlin's seventh.

What the audience didn't know was that he was in poor health. He had been on medication for many years following his heart attack in 1996. A month after the HBO broadcast, Carlin suffered another cardiac arrest. He was rushed him to Cedars-Sinai Medical Center in Los Angeles, where he told his daughter Kelly that he'd been experiencing symptoms for several months before the HBO performance but put off any medical care so that he could do it. For the stand-up comedian, Bishop Sheen was right: life was worth living.

In 2008, Carlin returned to the 1,600-seat Wells Fargo Center for the Arts in Santa Monica, California, for his fourteenth show, *It's Bad For Ya*. The original title was *The Parade of Useless Bullshit*. In an interview with Sonny Fox in 2006, Carlin says he had seventy-five minutes' worth of material in his computer, a series of short takes on a wide range of topics, including bureaucracy, overprotected children, and the myths of American patriotism. "I'm blessed with some pretty deep files. I don't suffer writer's block," he tells Fox. He created this show from scratch, including new thoughts on familiar subjects religion, big business, and death. He was a couple of months shy of his seventy-first birthday but ready to take to the stage after receiving more treatment for his heart.

"I'm an old fuck, not an old man or an old fart," proclaims Carlin at the start of his performance. "Old man is a point of view; a way of looking at things . . . I'm an old fuck . . . in this respect, 'fuck' is a synonym for 'fellow.'" Carlin celebrates his age and his place in the world. He looks older than seventy on this special, worn out by a heart that was failing him. Nevertheless, he's energized, present, and focussed. The theme of this show is death and how we deal with it spiritually, ethically, and personally. Carlin weaves a thread through his entire short takes in this performance. He first started talking about death back in 1977, "dying" versus "passing away." This time, perhaps it was intuitive that Carlin got personal.

The last quarter of the show reaches an important philosophical stage as Carlin waxes on "the glue that binds us as a nation: bullshit." He talks about the value of everything Americans hold dear: the rule of law, the Constitution, and the belief that the rituals surrounding these values are, in fact, bullshit. This includes removing your hat during the national anthem, swearing an oath on a Bible, and the empty phrase "God bless America," which closes every president's speech. "It's all bullshit and it's bad for ya," replies the sage.

Publicity photo for Carlin's last HBO special, It's Bad For Ya, *2008.* HBO/PHOTOFEST

George Carlin was at the top of his game on this, his final special. He would die three months later. But on this night in March, he had full control of his astute mind, a lifetime of experiences from which to draw, and the voice to deliver his ideas with perfect timing. "Artists grow, they're on a journey," he told Sonny Fox. "They don't know where it's going . . . [they] go through phases and changes . . . it's an ongoing thing."

Taken as a whole, the HBO specials reflect a developing career, one that ebbed and flowed with the times but never faded. George Carlin was proving to anyone who doubted him—the teachers in school, the U.S. Air Force captains, and the police in Milwaukee—that he was smarter, sharper, funnier, and more logical than any of them. He passed through the politically incorrect door that Lenny Bruce bravely opened, carving his own hilarious, thoughtful, and intuitive path. Carlin lived his dream because he was never asleep.

Fourteen

THE HALL OF FAMER

*A*t the American Comedy Awards in 2001, Garry Shandling gave George Carlin a lifetime achievement award. Shandling and Carlin had a lot in common: Carlin took the piss out of American ideals, Shandling took the piss out of show business glitz on the brilliant *Larry Sanders Show* on HBO. When the recipient, dressed in a tuxedo, came up to the stage to accept the award, he reflected on "the best job there is." Said Carlin, "You spend all day observing your fellow human beings and then at night, you go somewhere and tell them what worthless people they are." At the age of sixty-four, one of Carlin's most gracious fans bestowed him, perhaps a little early, with an honor marking his place in comedy history.

Shandling was the perfect choice. In the spring of 1969, he was an engineering student who wrote bits of comedy on the side. One day, he left his home in Tucson, Arizona, and traveled north 113 miles to Phoenix to see his first stand-up comedian, George Carlin. Carlin was performing at a jazz club called Mr. B's, and Shandling needed to see him. He showed up early, finding Carlin at the bar. Shandling rustled up some courage and introduced himself. He said he had written some monologues that he wanted Carlin to read. Shandling knew Carlin wrote his own material, but he took a chance and asked for some feedback. Carlin offered to read a couple of pieces, including one Shandling wrote about a commercial for the first marijuana cigarette. He invited Shandling to come back the next day.

Garry Shandling, 1987. Encouraged by Carlin to pursue writing, Shandling headed to LA after graduating from the University of Arizona. He never looked back. PHOTOFEST/FOX NETWORK

The following evening, Shandling made the two-hour drive back to Phoenix. He was feeling anxious. What would Carlin say about his work? He told Shandling that his stuff was raw but funny, encouraging him to write more. For Shandling, it was a life-changing endorsement money couldn't buy. After he graduated from the University of Arizona, he headed to Los Angeles to find work as a writer. Five years after this critical meeting, Shandling had three scripts accepted and produced for *Sanford & Son* before he hired an agent.

Awards notwithstanding, Shandling was grateful in a letter reproduced in *It's Garry Shandling's Book*, published by Random House in 2019. He thanks Carlin for being generous to him in Phoenix. He also says that he valued Carlin's honesty and disciplined work ethic. In the letter, he said that "he shared these values" and was inspired to pursue his dream of becoming a comedy writer. The letter was written in 1981 and never mailed. Twenty years later at the American Comedy Awards on April 14, 2001, Carlin praised Shandling as "one of the truly funny people to do this sort of thing," then his punch line, "but I do regret encouraging him at all."

It was a dark day in the comedy world when George Carlin died of heart failure on June 22, 2008. Tributes poured in. CNN's Larry King held a special TV vigil that evening with Lewis Black, Roseanne Barr, Jerry Seinfeld, and Bill Maher, sprinkled with plenty of Carlin bits. The Comedy Store in Hollywood changed its billboard with a simple message: "George Carlin, Rest in Peace." The *New York Times* had a great phrase in its obituary, noting that he "chafed society." Carlin the wordsmith would have approved. Ben Greenman said, "[Carlin] was the purest stage comedian of his generation . . . [He] kept the same look. He kept the same delivery. And he kept the same material, more or less, insisting, right up to the end, on puncturing political hypocrisy, deconstructing language, and taunting guardians of propriety" (*The New Yorker*, August 12, 2008).

A memorial service of around seventy people was held for Carlin about a week later at Jerry Hamza's house. Carlin wanted no public or religious service, and he also wanted to be cremated. He left specific instructions for a private wake with family and friends, his only other requests being rhythm and blues music and laughter, according to Kelly Carlin's memoir. Jack Burns, who made that all-important journey with Carlin to Hollywood in 1960, paid his respects. According to Kelly, "He stood up in the beautiful sunshine-filled backyard and started with, 'The family would like to thank you all for braving the brutal weather today' and got a huge laugh" (*A Carlin Home Companion*). Burns would die in 2020 at age eighty-six.

On May 12, 2020, the National Comedy Center hosted an event to celebrate Carlin's influence and unique contributions to comedy history. It was called "Laughing Matters: Carlin's Legacy." Hosted by Kelly Carlin to mark what would have been her father's eighty-third birthday, it took place in the early days of the COVID-19 pandemic, and its participants all gathered virtually via videoconference. While most of the remembrances were sentimental, they also had a common thread: that George Carlin was a master of stand-up comedy. Penn Jillette, of Penn & Teller, said that "his work ethic was incomparable" and in paying tribute said he didn't want to use the word "genius," so he didn't.

Merriam-Webster's Dictionary defines "legacy" as "something transmitted by or received from an ancestor or predecessor or from the past." When it comes to transmissions, George Carlin has few rivals. His books, HBO specials, and the albums he recorded are priceless. Another way to describe his impact as an artist is as a "ripple effect"—or, if you prefer, the "Carlin effect." It remains an important force in the zeitgeist. Bill Maher's "New Rules" segment has it. You hear it in Stephen Colbert's edgy, political monologues nightly. Patton Oswalt said that Carlin loomed "vast and thick over" his evolution as a stand-up comedian. Lewis Black stated to *Larry*

King Live, "He was vital to my growth, there's no denying it" (CNN, June 7, 2008).

During the Comedy Center tribute, Judd Apatow shared that the comedian's albums had held particular importance to him at a young age because "this is what being smart sounded like," adding that "it was a way of being skeptical about the world." In 2022, Apatow coproduced a two-part documentary about Carlin for HBO called *George Carlin's American Dream*. Tim Allen, comedian and actor, said that Carlin "found the common ground for all of us," including a personal note that "he made it possible to express myself." From Steven Wright to Judy Gold to Bill Engvall and Kathy Griffin, Carlin's special gift for "truth telling" inspired them to find their authentic selves.

In "Dying Is Hard, Comedy Is Harder," Jerry Seinfeld recalled his friendship with Carlin for the *New York Times*. It was published two days after Carlin died. His relationship with the man ran deep. He was struck by Carlin's funny perspective on life and the world around him, and he collected all of his albums. Seinfeld was impressed by Carlin's microworld observations and shaped his own act to reflect human behavior. Seinfeld stayed friends with Carlin right up until his untimely death. Carlin, likewise, loved Seinfeld for his keen ability to investigate the microworld—the human things we all know and experience.

*

Dennis Blair isn't the first person people think of when remembering George Carlin. But from 1990 to 2008, he had the auspicious duty of being Carlin's opening act. Blair was born in 1951 in Queens, New York. He cut his teeth as a musician first, learning guitar, singing, and composing his own songs. He was trying to model himself after the popular singer-songwriters of the early 1970s, like James Taylor and Cat Stevens. One night in 1979, before an inattentive audience,

Blair tried a parody of the Bee Gees song "Stayin' Alive," which was a hit record at the time. His version was called "Singing Too High." He made fun of the falsetto voices the brothers Gibb adopted: "Ah, Ah, Ah, Ah, singin' too high, singin' too high!" The audience ate it up. His act was just the right combination of joke telling and music satire, enough to get him a spot at New York's premier comedy club, Dangerfield's. He was a hit. Management asked him to open for veteran comedian Jackie Mason for a week. Then the club's owner, the one and only Rodney Dangerfield, hired Blair to open for him the following week.

Dangerfield, who took him under his wing and encouraged him to write his own stuff, mentored Blair. Blair wrote more song parodies, adding impressions of singers such as John Denver, Barbra Streisand, and Glen Campbell. He understood his role as the opening act: "I never go out there and say the audience is mine. It's always somebody else's." All he had to do was put the crowd in a good mood for the main act. Blair's moderate success soon had him opening for Dangerfield and Tom Jones. He got a spot on the *Tonight Show* in 1984 hosted by Joan Rivers, but the jobs were inconsistent, and Blair couldn't generate any momentum. So he and his wife moved to California in 1987 to try their luck on the West Coast.

A couple of years later, Blair couldn't believe his luck. In his wonderful memoir *Touring with Legends* (2021), Blair writes, "It all came out of the blue, as I sat in my den at home in Studio City, California . . . dreaming of landing a sitcom or a movie . . . with no work on the horizon." Then he got a call from his agent with the offer to open for Carlin, starting in Omaha, Nebraska, at the Orpheum Theater. It was an overwhelming experience for Blair: "I was about to open for the first time ever for this comedy genius . . . this was the equivalent of being a musical act and opening for someone like Bob Dylan." Despite his jitters, Blair's show went very well, and Carlin said so, telling the young comedian, "This was great. This is gonna work out." Blair was invited to dinner with Carlin and his manager, Jerry Hamza, becoming fast friends. For the next three months, they would hit the road and perform.

Blair and Carlin often drove from one show to another, part of Carlin's regional tours that avoided airports. On the *Yo Show* in 2021, Blair told Michael Yo that he and George would often talk about comedy and make up games and gags to amuse themselves "that were beyond R-rated." The two bonded over the years, as Blair fondly recalls in his autobiography. Carlin had several HBO specials under his belt, and he was taking care of his health: "It was amusing to me, when I hooked up with this counter-culture legendary guy, to witness him often ordering chicken with the skin cut off, pasta with no butter, and non-alcoholic beer."

When they toured, Blair described Carlin as a "hermit" locked in his hotel room, writing and crafting his next HBO show: "George was basically a private person . . . sequestering himself in his room and working, working, working on his next stand-up piece or HBO special." For Blair, who was asked to be Carlin's permanent opening act, it was hard to believe. "I began to hallucinate," he writes. Both Hamza and Carlin "agreed they liked me personally and that my act fit in well with George's show." A year later, Jerry Hamza became Blair's manager.

Blair's thirty-minute set each night was improvised. But after years of opening for Carlin, he got more serious about his preparation: "He's certainly improved my work ethic. I never used to sit down and write. I used to come up with everything onstage . . . I think I've become a little more satirical and edgy than I used to be, just because some of him has rubbed off on me" (*Pulse Weekly*, January 23, 2005). Now in his seventies, Blair tours as a headliner.

Maz Jobrani, who was born in Tehran, Iran, the same year as the release of *Class Clown*, tells the story of his first gig at the Comedy Store in West Hollywood. As an amateur, he was booked to perform in the Belly Room the same night as Carlin was performing on the main stage. He considered it an omen of things to come, and he was right. Carlin's approach to social issues was extremely important for him. He was free to talk about his experiences as an immigrant on the streets of Los Angeles with some funny results. Jobrani has released five TV specials and made appearances on the *Tonight Show with Jay Leno* and *WTF with Marc Maron*. In 2015, he released his autobiography *I'm Not a Terrorist, but I've Played One on TV: Memoirs of a Middle Eastern Funny Man*.

Russell Peters met Carlin in 1992. In his marvelous autobiography *Call Me Russell* (2010), the comedian tells a bizarre story of meeting Carlin in the middle of Toronto's Yonge Street the day the Toronto Blue Jays won their first World Series. He was among a river of people celebrating the event, and Peters couldn't believe he spotted his hero: "I was completely freaked out . . . I immediately ditched all my friends and worked my way against the throng of humanity, trying to catch up to Carlin. Next thing I knew, there he was right beside me." Peters says he walked Carlin through the crowd back to his hotel. It was an opportunity for him to talk to the master, and that's what Peters did, even inviting him to his mother's home for a meal of Indian food. (Carlin graciously declined.) Peters was a fledgling comedian at the time, barely three years into his shaky career, but he was determined to succeed. Peters said that Carlin told him to "get on stage as much as I could, wherever I could . . . he put it in my head that night, at such a young age, that comedy was a craft, that is something you could actually get better at with practice." Peters had the impetus to work harder on his act, and he did it by picking up gigs everywhere he could, be it a party, an amateur night, or a nightclub intermission.

Peters was raised in the culturally diverse city of Brampton, Ontario. He broke out in 2003 on the half-hour series *Comedy Now!*, based on his life growing up as an "Anglo-Indian." A fan uploaded it to YouTube in 2004, pulling in millions of viewers. Peters had landed. He played Harlem's Apollo Theater in 2005 and made his *Tonight Show* debut three years later. In 2007, following the Carlin edict, Peters was asked to host at the Hermosa Beach Comedy and Magic Club. It was a personal highlight. Carlin was on the bill to perform material for what would be his last HBO special, *It's Bad for Ya*. In his book, Peters includes a backstage photo with Carlin.

"That's the job. That's what I want to do," exclaimed Jim McAleese after the nineteen-year-old traveled to Toronto to see George Carlin in performance. He was at the O'Keefe Centre (now Meridian Hall) in August 1972, days after Carlin's arrest in Milwaukee and mere months before the release of *Class Clown*. In 2020, McAleese recalled the show and his epiphany on the podcast *Comedy Album Book Club*. Carlin's performance was material from his latest album, set for release in September. McAleese was amazed by Carlin's new routine, dressed in jeans and tie-dyed shirt, bearded, with nothing but a microphone and bar stool on the stage. Inspired but slow to

Bill Maher on Real Time, *HBO. His segment* New Rules, *captures the ripple of Carlin's influence.* HBO/PHOTOFEST

start, McAleese took seven years to land a gig at Mark Breslin's Yuk Yuk's club in Toronto, the premier comedy club back then. Within six months, he was headlining because "there was lots of room for comics in those days."

McAleese didn't adopt the Carlin style of humor; he had a clean act full of Canadian references and impersonations. What he did learn from Carlin was a formula for success: get a laugh every third line. When *Class Clown* was released, McAleese had a copy of the show he witnessed, declaring that Carlin's presentation at that time "had to be heard, not seen. [Carlin] eases people in with low brow humor to gain their trust for the deeper, higher commentary." He and his friends played the album up to ten times a week, learning the bits like songs from a favorite pop record. "Comics are questioners," says McAleese, currently a teacher at Second City in Toronto.

*

In 2008, not long before his death, George Carlin was named a recipient of the Mark Twain Prize for "people who have had an impact on American society in ways similar to the distinguished 19th century novelist and essayist." The first comedian to get the award had been Richard Pryor in 1998. Carlin was the tenth. He learned of the news about a week before he died and appreciated the honor. "Thank you Mr. Twain. Have your people call my people" (*Daily Variety*, June 19, 2008).

Consequently, the televised ceremony on November 10 in front of a packed Kennedy Center became a memorial. At the event were Carlin's brother Patrick, his daughter Kelly, and Sally Wade. The tributes were personal and hilarious, as the show turned into a wake for the Irish comic, featuring speeches from Jerry Seinfeld, Garry Shandling, Joan Rivers, Jon Stewart, Margaret Cho, and Lewis Black. *USA*

Today reported that protesters were a couple of blocks away carrying signs that read, "God Hates Carlin!"

Bill Maher said he was moved by Carlin's second album, *FM&AM*, marking the comedian's transition from jester to poet through reinvention: "[It] inspired me to believe that I could do things differently." Of Carlin's last HBO special, *It's Bad for Ya*, Maher was in awe: "Damn! He is still the rabbit and I don't know if anybody's going to catch him, not in the terms and the currency I value most: utter honesty." Maher's documentary *Religulous* cruises on the Carlin ripple. As he told Larry King on CNN in 2008, "Carlin was the only guy who talked about religion . . . where I got my courage to do it."

Two years later, on March 24, 2010, at another memorial hosted by the New York Public Library, Lewis Lapham, former publisher of *Harper's*, put Twain and Carlin into perfect context: "Knowing that liberty has ambitious and devoted enemies, Carlin, like Twain and [Ambrose] Bierce and Lenny Bruce also knew that the survival of the American democracy depends less on the size of its armies than on the capacity of its individual citizens to rely, if only momentarily, on the strength of their own minds. He [Carlin] sent his humor on a moral errand, what Twain called painted fire, intended to preserve his fellow Americans from being shriveled into sheep."

In 2015, Carlin's image joined the National Portrait Gallery in Washington, D.C., dedicated to "Americans who have influenced politics, history and culture." When it made the news, his daughter Kelly told NPR in 2015, "I know he would have been thrilled, even though he was a man who stood up against all of our major institutions in this country," adding that "there's a small part of him that wanted to always kind of prove how clever and smart he was to these institutions, and the fact that they give him a little nod every once in a while, he always, always enjoyed." The black-and-white photograph by Arthur Grace, taken in 1990, features Carlin in an expressive mid-pose during one of his routines onstage. It captures his energy and playfulness beautifully. The portrait is in fine company. Carlin's childhood heroes Fred Allen, Danny Kaye, and the Marx Brothers are in the gallery, as are his contemporaries Lenny Bruce and Richard Pryor.

In 2016 at the National Comedy Center in Jamestown, New York, the archives of George Carlin were opened to the public. Fully digitized versions of Carlin's own handwritten notes make up a special

A place for his stuff. ZUMA PRESS / ALAMY STOCK PHOTO

room inside. His daughter Kelly collected all of her father's notes about words: rhymes, oxymorons, phrases, slang—anything that had to do with the English language that fascinated him. She donated them to the museum, a first-rate cathedral of comedy. By digitizing the notes in Carlin's own hand, the center created a living, interactive window into his process. On their website, a short montage is available featuring Carlin's handwritten notes. The collection is remarkable: some 2,000 topic files on everything from cats to war preserved for all to see.

It's a gift for the ages.

Complete Works

Books

Sometimes a Little Brain Damage Can Help 1984 (Running Press)
Brain Droppings 1998 (Hyperion)
Napalm & Silly Putty 2001 (Hyperion)
When Will Jesus Bring the Pork Chops? 2004 (Hyperion)
Three Times Carlin: An Orgy of George 2006 (Hyperion)
Last Words, a Memoir (with Tony Hendra) 2009 (Free Press)

Albums

Burns and Carlin at the Playboy Club Tonight 1963 (ERA Records)
Take-Offs and Put-Ons 1966 (RCA)
FM & AM 1972 (Little David Records)
Class Clown 1972 (Little David Records)
Occupation: Foole 1973 (Little David Records)
Toledo Window Box 1974 (Little David Records)
An Evening with Wally Londo, Featuring Bill Slaszo 1975 (Little David Records)
On the Road 1977 (Little David Records)
Killer Carlin 1981 (LAFF Records) (reissue of Burns and Carlin)
A Place for My Stuff 1981 (Atlantic)
Carlin on Campus 1984 (Eardrum)

Playin' with Your Head 1986 (Eardrum)
What Am I Doing in New Jersey? 1988 (Eardrum/Atlantic)
Parental Advisory: Explicit Lyrics 1990 (Atlantic/Laugh)
Jammin' in New York 1992 (Eardrum/Atlantic)
Back in Town 1996 (Atlantic)
You Are All Diseased 1999 (Eardrum)
Complaints and Grievances 2001 (Eardrum/Atlantic)
Life Is Worth Losing 2006 (Eardrum/Atlantic)
It's Bad for Ya 2008 (Eardrum/Atlantic)
I Kinda Like It When a Lotta People Die 2016 (Eardrum/MPI
   Media)

Compilations

Indecent Exposure 1978 (Atlantic Records)
Classic Gold 1992 (Atlantic)
The Little David Years [1971–1977] 1999 (Atlantic)

Singles (7-inch promos) (Little David Records, unless otherwise indicated)

11 O'clock News 1972
FM & AM (excerpts) EP 1972
Laugh Your Ass Off (promotional EP featuring Carlin, Avery and
   Schreiber, and The Committee 1973
Occupation: Foole EP 1973
Toledo Window Box EP 1974
An Evening with Wally Londo, Featuring Bill Slaszo EP 1975
New News Is Good News 1975
Edited for Air Play EP 1977
Head Lines 1977
Seven Words You Can Never Say on Television (radio edit) 1978
From the Atlantic LP, *A Place for My Stuff* (12-inch EP) 1981

HBO Specials

On Location: George Carlin at USC 1977
George Carlin: Again! 1978
Carlin at Carnegie 1983
Carlin on Campus 1984
Playin' with Your Head 1986
What Am I Doing in New Jersey? 1988
Doin' It Again 1990
Jammin' in New York 1992
Back in Town 1996
George Carlin: 40 Years of Comedy 1997 (with Jon Stewart)
You Are All Diseased 1999
Complaints and Grievances 2001
Life Is Worth Losing 2006
It's Bad for Ya 2008

Audiobooks

Brain Droppings 2000
Napalm & Silly Putty 2001
More Napalm & Silly Putty 2002
George Carlin Reads to You 2004
Last Words (abridged) read by Patrick Carlin 2009

Motion Pictures

With Six You Get Egg Roll 1966
Car Wash 1976
Americathon 1979
Outrageous Fortune 1987
Bill & Ted's Excellent Adventure 1989

Working Trash 1990
Bill & Ted's Bogus Journey 1991
The Prince of Tides 1991
Dogma 1999
Jay and Silent Bob Strike Back 2001
Scary Movie 3 2003
Jersey Girl 2004
Tarzan 2: The Legend Begins 2005
Cars 2006
Happily N'Ever After 2006
Thomas & Friends: Halloween Adventures 2006

Television

That Girl 1966
Tony Orlando and Dawn 1976
Welcome Back, Kotter 1977
Disneyland 1988
Bill & Ted's Excellent Adventures (TV series) 1990
The George Carlin Show 1994–1995
Shining Time Station 1995
Streets of Laredo (miniseries) 1995
Thomas the Tank Engine & Friends 1984–1995
Storytime with Thomas 1999
MADtv 2000

Bibliography

Book, Michael. *Book on Acting: Improvisation Technique.* Beverly Hills, CA: Silman-James Press, 2002.

Brennan, Bill. *George Carlin's Alter-Ego.* Monroe, CT: Quaesitum Publishers, 2009.

Brown, David Jay. *Conversations on the Edge of the Apocalypse.* New York: Palgrave Macmillan, 2005.

Carlin, Kelly. *A Carlin Home Companion: Growing Up with George.* New York: St. Martin's Press, 2015.

Carlin, George. *3 x Carlin: An Orgy of George.* New York: Hyperion, 2006.

Carlin, George (with Tony Hendra). *Last Words: A Memoir.* New York: Free Press, 2009.

Cook, Kevin. *Flip: The Inside Story of TV's First Black Superstar.* New York: Viking, 2013.

Curtis, James. *Last Man Standing: Mort Sahl and the Birth of Modern Comedy.* Jackson: University Press of Mississippi, 2017.

Douglas, Mike (with Thomas Kelly and Michael Heaton). *I'll Be Right Back.* New York: Simon & Schuster, 2000.

Gold, Judy. *Yes, I Can Say That.* New York: Dey Street, 2020.

Goldman, Albert (from the journalism of Lawrence Schiller). *Ladies and Gentlemen, Lenny Bruce!* New York: Ballantine Books, 1974.

Kleeblatt, Norman, ed. *Action/Abstraction: Pollock, de Kooning, and American Art, 1940–1976.* New Haven, CT: Yale University Press, 2008.

Koestler, Arthur. *The Act of Creation.* London: Picador, 1974.

Krassner, Paul. *Confessions of a Raving, Unconfined Nut*. Berkeley, CA: Soft Skull Press, 2012.

Leno, Jay (with Bill Zehme). *Leading with My Chin*. New York: Harper-Collins, 1996.

McWhorter, John H. *Nine Nasty Words: English in the Gutter: Then, Now, and Forever*. New York: Avery, 2021.

Nesteroff, Kliph. *The Comedians*. New York: Grove Press, 2015.

Peters, Russell. *Call Me Russell*. Toronto: Doubleday Canada, 2010.

Saul, Scott. *Becoming Richard Pryor*. New York: Harper Perennial, 2015.

Steinberg, David. *Inside Comedy: The Soul, Wit, and Bite of Comedy and Comedians of the Last Five Decades*. New York: Alfred A. Knopf, 2021.

Stonehill, Judith, ed. *Greenwich Village Stories: A Collection of Memories*. New York: Universal Publishing, 2014.

Sullivan, James. *7 Dirty Words: The Life and Crimes of George Carlin*. Cambridge, MA: Da Capo Press, 2010.

Tropiano, Stephen, *Saturday Night Live FAQ*. Milwaukee, WI: Applause Books, 2013.

Vonnegut, Kurt, and Susanne McConnell. *Pity The Reader: On Writing with Style*. New York: Rosetta Books, 2019. (ebook version)

Wade, Sally. *The George Carlin Letters*. New York: Gallery Books, 2011.

Whitaker, Mark. *Cosby: His Life and Times*. New York: Simon & Schuster, 2014.

Zoglin, Richard, *Comedy at the Edge*. New York: Bloomsbury, 2008.

Periodicals

Gallery, Vol. 1, No. 7, May 1973.

Harris, Paul. "Carlin makes Twain grade." *Daily Variety*, June 19, 2008.

Harris, Paul. "Carlin toasted at Twain Prize fete." *Daily Variety*, November 12, 2008.

Maryles, Daisy. "Carlin drops in on the charts." *Publishers Weekly*, June 8, 1998, 20.

Maryles, Daisy. "Bringing home the bacon." *Publishers Weekly*, November 1, 2004, 16.

Milwaukee Journal, July 22, 1972.

Milwaukee Sentinel, July 22, 1972.

National Lampoon, March/April 1994.

Newark Evening News, September 9, 1963 .

New York Times, January 21, 1992.

Playboy, Vol. 9, No. 1, January 1962.

Playboy, Vol. 29, No. 1, January 1982.

Riley, Jenelle. "Catching up with Tom Papa." *Back Stage West*, February 26, 2004, 15.

The Realist, Issue No. 83, October 1968 [Transcript of the CBC program *The Way It Is* with Marshall McLuhan originally broadcast on CBLT.]

Rolling Stone, Issue No. 115, August 17, 1972.

Winnipeg Free Press, May 23, 1986.

Wloszczyna, Susan. "George Carlin: A legacy to look up to." *USA Today*, November 11, 2008.

Websites

http://data.perseus.org/citations/urn:cts:greekLit:tlg0086.tlg025.perseus-engl:1.982b

https://www.theatlantic.com/culture/archive/2021/09/911-comedy-too-soon/620036

https://www.cablecenter.org/programs/the-hauser-oral-history-project/f-listings/michael-fuchs.html

https://constitutioncenter.org/blog/george-carlin-and-the-supreme-court-36-years-later

https://live-cdn-www.nypl.org/s3fs-public/av/transcripts/LIVECarlin_3.24Transcript.pdf

https://www.nytimes.com/2021/10/26/arts/television/mort-sahl-dead.html

https://georgecarlin.com

http://www.georgecarlin.net (Fan site curated by "Bill")

http://www.henrybwalthall.com

https://hometownbyhandlebar.com/?p=34435

https://www.imdb.com/name/nm0137506/bio?ref_=nm_dyk_qt
_sm#quotes

https://jaydixit.com

https://lennybruce.org

https://www.latimes.com/opinion/la-oew-allcroft26-2008jun26-story.html

https://www.youtube.com/watch?v=qUimkYcASmo (*Yo Show* podcast,
August 19, 2021. Host, Michael Yo.)

https://solarsystem.nasa.gov/solar-system/oort-cloud/in-depth

https://www.npr.org/2015/03/02/390245038/ben-franklins-famous-liberty
-safety-quote-lost-its-context-in-21st-century

https://www.onmilwaukee.com

http://www.ep.tc/realist/index.html

https://www.reddit.com/r/GeorgeCarlin/comments/kxjzcm/a_picture_of
_george_carlin_his_wife_brenda_carlin

https://reelinintheyears.com

https://www.televisionacademy.com

https://www.thestar.com/entertainment/2009/01/22/fbi_files_on_george
_carlin_silent_on_his_famous_seven_words.html

http://uncledir.blogspot.com (Bob Altman)

https://www.youtube.com/watch?v=s-clvDxl8qI (Sonny Fox show 2006,
Sirius XM)

Documentary Films

I Am Richard Pryor. Network Entertainment/Thunderbird, 2019.

The Subversive Humor of Lenny Bruce. Presented by Barry Sanders, Chicago Humanities Festival, 2009.

Too Soon: Comedy After 9/11. Nick Scown and Julie Seabaugh, directors.

Radio/Television

A&E Biography. *George Carlin: More Than 7 Words*, April 12, 2000, CBS News Productions.

"Comedian George Carlin Is National Portrait Gallery's Newest Face." *All Things Considered*, March 27, 2015.

Inside The Actors Studio, October 31, 2004, Season 11, Episode 4, Bravo.

Late Late Show with Tom Snyder, CBS.

INDEX